CONFEDERATE GUNS

AND THEIR CURRENT PRICES

Illustrated handbook that lists, describes and gives up-to-date values of all the known hand guns and shoulder firearms made or used by the Confederacy in the War between the States.

PLUS—Directory of Confederate Edged Weapons—Swords, Sabers, Bayonets, Bowie Knives—Makers, Dealers, Importers.

BY MARTIN RYWELL

———

ELEVENTH EDITION

———

PIONEER PRESS — UNION CITY, TENNESSEE

AUTHOR'S NOTE

MY SINCERE GRATITUDE AND APPRECIATION to the following to whom I am indebted for the loan of the photographs reproduced in this book: William A. Albaugh 3rd of Richmond, Va.; Valmore Forgett of Clemson, S. C.; Carroll C. Holloway of Longview, Texas; Paul C. Janke of Houston, Texas; the Smithsonian Institution and J. T. Cotton.

The prices as set down in this guide represent a screening of the sales records throughout the nation. Since very few specimens of some Confederate guns are known, these prices are open to controversy. Then again many variables enter into the price. The author does not claim to be infallible. He does know that enough checking and digging has been done through a good many years to make sure that he has arrived at a complete, accurate and fair guide. The prices are therefore submitted as a means of comparison and should be used with an open mind. Elasticity of value is governed by scarcity, demand and condition. That is the economic yardstick. These guns besides their badges of service and dignity of age are also bound by sentimental and family ties to their proud owners. We cannot standardize values nor do we wish to. All we hope for is that this book serve as a helpful aid.

MARTIN RYWELL.

Other Books by Pioneer Press

AMERICAN ANTIQUE PISTOLS AND THEIR CURRENT PRICES

U. S. MILITARY MUSKETS, RIFLES, CARBINES AND THEIR CURRENT PRICES

AMERICAN ANTIQUE RIFLES AND THEIR CURRENT PRICES

CONFEDERATE GUNS AND THEIR CURRENT PRICES

COLT TIPS

AMERICAN HANDMADE KNIVES OF TODAY

SOUTHERN DERRINGERS OF THE MISSISSIPPI VALLEY

SKETCHBOOK '76

THE STORY OF FIREARMS IGNITIONS

A BRIEF HISTORY OF BULLET MOULDS

VOLCANIC FIREARMS—AND THEIR SUCCESSORS

GUN COLLECTORS GUIDE

CARTRIDGE MANUEL

TENNESSEE COOK BOOK

SHARPS RIFLE THE GUN THAT SHAPED AMERICAN DESTINY

CONFEDERATE COOK BOOK

CIVIL WAR MILITARY DICTIONARY

THE POWDER FLASK

AMERICAN NICKEL-PLATED REVOLVER

CONTENTS

~

ILLUSTRATIONS

INDEX

CONFEDERATE GUNS

By Martin Rywell

HUSHED IS THE ROLL OF THE REBEL DRUM, nought is left except the splendid record of their valor. That record of valor is heightened by the knowledge of the shortage of firearms. So desperate did the shortage of arms eventually become that about 2500 pikes were given to the soldiers to use in repelling Sherman's army as it marched through Georgia.

Brooks tells of an old man living in Kentucky during the Secession War that had two sons; one enlisted in the Confederate Army and the other in the United States Army. Within twelve months one was brought home dead, and within a short time the other was brought home like his brother, having also been killed in battle. Both were placed in his garden side by side and this inscription was placed upon the monument: "God alone knows which was right."

NO OTHER WAR has been studied so minutely and restudied as the Civil War or the War between the States. The name of the war as well as the difference between the label of a rebel and a patriot was determined by the conclusion of the conflict.

So much led to the war and so much followed from it that it is the crucial event in our history. "For the number of men involved, the amount of space traversed, the coast line blockaded, of material consumed and results achieved," writes M. B. Greenbie, "it exceeded all wars up to that time." From 1868 to 1900 every man elected President except one, had been an officer in the Union Army.

The North had 23 states with a population of 22 millions and industrial wealth. The South had 11 states with 9 million population, of which 3½ millions were slaves.

There were about 2½ million men in both armies. More than 600,000 lost their lives or more Americans were killed in it than in the American forces in both World War 1 and 2 combined.

There were 57 varieties of guns used in the Confederacy with about as many variations. These may be divided into five broad classifications. In the first category the Confederates used the United States regulation arms that were in the armories and arsenals when they took possession. In this class are included abandoned state armories that were reactivated at the onset of the war. An armory is devoted to the manufacture of arms and an arsenal is used for the storage and issuance of arms though an armory may have a repair shop.

The second category was the private arms with Confederate markings. The third category was the arms imported from abroad. The fourth category was arms captured. The fifth category was arms manufactured.

The first category was the United States regulation arms of many descriptions up to Model 1861. (Consult Rywell's U. S. Military Muskets, Carbines and Rifles for detailed list.) The capture of Harper's Ferry Armory by the Confederacy on April 18, 1861, was a vital victory even though the Federals fired and partially destroyed it. A Confederate report read, "I have examined some of the 14,000 arms that were burned in the Armory and find I can make serviceable guns of them." It was a vital victory, not because of the salvage of the small amount of arms, but because of the machinery and supplies. The machinery was transported to and installed at Richmond, Virginia and Fayetteville, North Carolina.

We may include in this category the state armories such as the Virginia Manufactory Armory at Richmond and the Palmetto Armory at Columbia, South Carolina, where many old guns reposed. Some of these were altered and some simply received Confederate identification marks.

The alteration in the main was conversion from flintlock to percussion. In 1843 the United States adopted the percussion ignition system (Britain in 1836) and ordered the alteration of all flintlock arms, though the work was not completed until 1848. Several hundred thousand arms were altered. Another alteration was to shorten the barrel length.

The Virginia Manufactory was a Virginia state enterprise organized in 1802 for the manufacture of all types of military equipment and reactivated in 1860 for weapon alteration.

It converted the Virginia Manufactory Pistol from flintlock to percussion. It was caliber 69, single shot, 12½ inch barrel, steel ramrod with lockplate marked rear of hammer "Virginia Manufactory, Richmond plus year (1805 to 1809)." Sometimes the name of a private gunsmith who altered the ignition was added.

Virginia also issued the Rappahannock Forge Pistol after alteration to percussion. It was the first military pistol manûfactured in this country. Rappahannock Forge was set up before 1776 by James Hunter and manufactured pistols and muskets for the Virginia Convention. It was caliber 65, single shot, 8¾ inch barrel marked, "J. Hunter." It had a brass butt plate, trigger guard, thimble and an iron ramrod. At the rear of the cock on the lockplate was marked, "Rapa Forge."

Thus we find in southern arsenals when the war began only a few hundred antiquated horse pistols mainly of flintlock ignition.

C. Dimmick, Virginia's Chief of Ordnance in November 1861 reported: "This state has issued 10,000 U. S. flintlocks which she received from the Federal Government years ago. These have no distinctive mark, and therefore cannot be recognized as belonging to this State . . . Virginia has issued 10,000 percussion muskets, United States, and 50,000 Virginia flintlock muskets, these last plainly known by the stamp "Virginia" upon the lock . . . I understand that a number of Virginia manufactured muskets made at the Armory here many years ago, and have been issued from this department, are being gathered into the Confederate Ordnance Department to be altered into percussion."

The Palmetto Armory was established in 1852 when secession threatened and the firm of Boatwright & Glaze (William Glaze and Company) received a contract for 24,000 arms (muskets, rifles, pistols). Machinery was purchased and arms are dated 1852 and 1853 but the exact number manufactured is unknown. The Palmetto Armory was reactivated for the repair of arms. South Carolina issued the Palmetto Armory Pistol manufactured in 1852. It was caliber 54 percussion, single shot, 8½ inch barrel marked, "William Glaze & Co. V. P. 1852," and the lockplate marked, "Palmetto Armory, Columbia, S. C. 1852" with a Palmetto tree. This pistol was a copy of the United States Model 1842 pistol.

Texas had a quantity of old flintlock guns, a gift of the Federal government to the Texas militia after the Mexican War. The Austin Armory altered them to percussion.

This category of arms is not primarily within our province since they are difficult to identify and identification is not very dependable.

The second category was the private arms enlisted into the service altered, and stamped with Confederate identification marks. The alteration was to bore and rifle for caliber 58 ammunition; to fit for bayonets or to cut down to carbine size. Samuel Sutherland of Richmond had the principal shop for such alterations though many similar ones were scattered throughout the Confederacy. Tennessee due to either the contribution of numerous hog rifles or the number of skilled gunsmiths abounded in such alteration shops which included Memphis, Murfreesboro, Nashville and Pulaski.

In 1862 the following law was enacted in the Confederacy:

"That each man who may be mustered into service, and who shall arm himself with a musket, shotgun, rifle or carbine, accepted as an efficient weapon, shall be paid the value thereof, to be ascertained by the mustering officer under such regulations as may be prescribed by the Secretary of War, if he is willing to sell the same, and if he is not, then he shall be entitled to receive $1.00 a month for the use of said received and approved musket, rifle, shotgun or carbine."

Thus privately owned firearms were received into service and altered for military use.

The third category was the arms that were imported from abroad.

Judah Benjamin, Secretary of War, reported to President Jefferson in March 1862:

"I know of no legislation which could aid the Department in procuring a supply of small-arms. Nearly every mechanic in the Confederacy competent to manufacture small-arms is believed to be engaged in the work ... When it is considered that the Government of the United States—with all its accumulation of arms for half a century, and all its workshops and arsenals, public and private, and its untrammeled intercourse with foreign nations—has recently been compelled to disband a number of calvary regiments on account of the difficulty of arming them, and has been driven to the necessity of making purchases of arms in Europe in very large quantities, and of saltpeter by thousands of tons, some faint idea may be formed of the difficulties against which this Department has been and is now struggling in the effort to furnish arms and munitions for our troops.

"The difficulty is not in the want of legislation. Laws cannot suddenly convert farmers into gunsmiths. Our people are not artisans, except to a very limited degree. In the very armory here at Richmond the production could be greatly increased if skilled labor could be procured. In the absence of home manufactures no recourse remains but importation, and with our commerce substantially at an end with foreign nations the means of importation are limited."

Captain Lardner Gibbon, Inspector of Ordnance at Richmond observed that better guns could be bought abroad than could be found at home and mentioned good rifles from the London Arms Manufacturing Company and from Liege, Belgium. He doubtless intended the London Armoury Company of London.

Some of the prominent dealer-importers in the South were: Canfield Brothers and Company of Baltimore; Courtney and Tennent of Charleston, South Carolina; W. B. & C. Fisher of Lynchburg, Virginia; Hallmann and Taylor of Montgomery, Alabama; Hyde and Goodrich of New Orleans succeeded by Thomas, Griswold and Company; T. W. Radcliffe of Columbia, South Carolina; Schneider & Glassick of Memphis, Tennessee; and Samuel Sutherland; Mitchell and Tyler; Kent, Paine and Company, all of Richmond, Virginia. Their name was usually stamped on the arm they imported.

The Tranter revolver was imported from England and widely used in the South prior to the war. They bear the names of the importers which were Hyde and Goodrich, A. B. Griswold and Company, T. W. Radcliffe and others.

During the war the following revolvers were imported from England: They were Adams, percussion ignition, caliber 44, 5 shots, Deane, caliber 44, 5 shot, frame marked, "Patent 5553." Kerr, caliber 44, 5 shot, frame marked "Kerr's Patent 9224" and the Tranter Caliber 36 or 44, 6 shot, and frame marked "Tranter Patent." They were manufactured by the London Armoury Company. From France came some pinfire revolvers and the LeMat. While the LeMat was an import it was the invention of a Southerner and will be included in a distinct division.

The Adams, Deane, Kerr, and Tranter Revolvers are each worth about $125.00, dependent upon condition.

The North imported the following revolvers from France and it is possible that the South also bought some.

Devisme caliber 36, 6 shot, percussion.

Houllier & Blanchard, caliber 44, 6 shot percussion.

Lefaucheux, caliber about 42 pinfire. These were bought in very large quantities.

Perrin caliber 44, metallic cartridge.

Raphael caliber 42, 6 shot, metallic cartridge center fire.

Cartridge revolvers were emerging. The Smith and Wesson Model No. 1 22 caliber r.f., 7 shot had been manufactured from 1857 to 1860. In June 1861 Smith & Wesson brought out their Model 1½ with a caliber 32 copper cased cartridge. This new 6 shot weapon became very popular because it could be loaded quickly and its ammunition was waterproof but it waned mainly because of the inability to obtain cartridges. The caliber was not effective enough and after prolonged shooting the powder fouling gummed the action because of too much tolerance between the cylinder and the frame top strap. The revolvers purchased by the North were the Allen & Wheelock, Beal, Colt, Joslyn, Pettingill, Remington, Rogers and Spencer, Savage, Starr, and Whitney. It was the first major conflict in which revolvers were used extensively.

The following shoulder arms were imported exclusive of LeMat Revolving Carbine.

WILSON BREECH-LOADING RIFLE

Cal. 56, bbl. 33, has cutlass bayonet, brass butt plate, trigger guard and tip. Lockplate "Crown 1863" bbl. m. "p.m." breech block m. "T. Wilson's Patent."—$250.00—

WHITWORTH RIFLE

Cal. 45, bb. 33, iron mounted, checkered stock, lockplate, "Whitworth Rifle Co., Manchester," bbl.m. 'Whitworth Patent." Used as sharpshooter rifle.—$300.00—

TERRY BOLT-ACTION CARBINE

Cal. 54, bbl. 25, iron mounted, concealed cap box in stock, ramrod lockplate, "Thomas Blissett," breech m. "Terry's Patent 30 bore." bbl. "Thomas Blissett," Liverpool.—$250.00—

Cal. 54, bbl. 24", no concealed cap box or ramrod. Lockplate, "Crown" plus "V. R. Tower, 1875," breech "C. S. bbl. "Terry's Patent."—$250.00—

KERR RIFLE

Cal. 44, bbl 37, iron mounted. Lockplate m. "L. A. Co. 1863" breech m. "Kerr's Patent" "L. A. Co."—$275.00—

ENFIELD RIFLE OFFICERS MODEL

Cal. 577, bbl. 39", brass mounted; iron bands, adjustable rear sight. Lockplate, "L. A. Co. 1861 plus Crown V. R.," bbl. m. "L. A. C." plus p.m., stock stamped "London Armory Bermondsey 1861."—$275.00—

ENFIELD CARBINE

Cal. 577, bbl. 21, swivel ramrod; brass mounted lockplate "Barnet, London, Tower plus Crown."—$225.00—

ENFIELD RIFLED MUSKETOON

Cal. 577, bbl. 23, two-leaf sight. Lockplate, "Barnett, London."—$225.00—

ENFIELD SHORT PATTERN RIFLE

Cal. 577, bbl. 33, butt plate, trigger guard, and stock tip are of brass; bbl. blued. Lockplate "Tower 1861 plus Crown V. R."—$250.00—

ENFIELD RIFLE MODEL 1858

Cal. 577, bbl. 39", brass mounted; iron bands, adjustable rear sight. Lockplate "Tower 1862 plus Crown." bbl. British p.m.—$250.00—

BRUNSWICK RIFLE

Cal. 704, twist bbl., brass mountings and patch box; back-action lock, adjustable leaf sight. Lockplate "Manufactory Enfield V. R. plus Crown plus 1842" bbl. British proof mark.—$250.00—

BRITISH TOWER MUSKET

Cal. 753, bbl. 39, percussion; brass but plate, trigger guard, stock tip, three ramrod tubes. Lockplate m. "Tower" with Crown. bbl. has Birmingham proof marks.—$250.00—

BRITISH SHARPSHOOTER'S RIFLE

Cal. 45, bbl. 36, 3" octagon, 33" round, engraved iron mounted; half cock safety lock; checkered stock; bbl. m. "Henry's Patent Rifling" plus p.m.—$300.00—

AUSTRIAN RIFLE

Cal. 54, bbl. 33, back-action lock, 2 band.—$225.00—

In this category of imports from abroad we may include arms purchased in the North. During late 1859 and in 1860 many arms were purchased from the United States government and Northern manufacturers. Purchases from Northern manufacturers continued after Jefferson Davis was elected President of the Confederate States on February 9, 1861. John Forsyth and other agents continued to make purchases in the North. On April 19, 1861 an embargo on shipment of arms to the Southern states was declared. In November 1861 Major Ben McCulloch obtained 1000 Colt revolvers for the State of Texas. Delivery became difficult but as late as March 1863 we find the following communication. "I am informed that carbines and pistols can be had; bought in New York and shipped to Brownsville (Texas) without trouble. Am offered 5,000 Colt's revolvers at $25.00 for the Navy size and $38.00 for the Army size."

Mississippi entered into a contract June 6, 1860 for 1500 rifles with Eli Whitney though it was later cancelled when the 60 sample arms were not up to specifications. (See Whitney—Miss. Rifle.) This was indicative of the arms buying by southern states. Alabama during the latter part of 1860 purchased 9,500 arms (muskets, rifles, carbines.)

The fourth category was arms captured. General Gorgas reported that for the year ending September 30, 1864 the Confederacy imported 30,000 small arms, manufactured 20,000 and captured 45,000. With reference to the number captured he adds, "The captures have been about 45,000 and the losses about 30,000, leaving a gain of 15,000."

Many of the captured arms were sent to the Confederate States Armory at Richmond and Solomon Adams, Master Armorer of Virginia reported (Sept. 22, 1864):

"Among the old arms received in this armory for repairs during the current month I have noticed the above arms from a variety of manufacturing establishments, all of them made after the U. S. '55 model and all interchanging with the Richmond rifle musket except in lock plate and mainspring, which have been altered in the Northern Arms.

I suppose there are in the north (including breech-loading) not less than thirty-eight armories, all on a large scale, and their total product probably will not fall short of 5,000 arms per day.

I beg to present for your information a list of rifle muskets manufactured North, and their places of manufacture:

Springfield U. S. rifle, Springfield, Mass.

Philadelphia U. S. rifle, Philadelphia, Pa.

Bridesburg U. S. rifle, Bridesburg, Pa.

Park, Snow & Co. U. S. rifle, Meriden, Conn.

Colt U. S. rifle, Hartford, Conn.

Whitney U. S. rifle, Whitneyville, Conn.

Wm. Muir & Co. U. S. rifle, Windsor Locks, Conn.

Norwich U. S. rifle, Norwich, Conn.

L. G. & Y. U. S. rifle, Windsor, Vermont.

Providence Tool Company U. S. rifle, Providence, R. I.

E. Robinson U. S. rifle, New York.

U. A. Co. U. S. rifle, New York.

Remington U. S. rifle, Ilion, N. Y.

Watertown U. S. rifle, Watertown, Mass.

Wm. Mason U. S. rifle, Taunton, Mass.

Eagleville Company U. S. rifle, place not known.

Norfolk U. S. rifle, Norfolk, Va."

Confederate firearm machinery and parts came from the capture and removal of the Harper's Ferry Armory and Arsenal.

We have listed the U. S. regulation arms obtained by seizure of U. S. forts and arsenals under the first category of possession rather than under fourth category of capture because the property was all located within the bounds of the Confederate states and the North did not attempt to protect the property or prevent seizure.

The fifth category was the arms manufactured in the Confederacy with the limited available means.

In August 1861 the Ordnance office of the Confederate War Department stated:

"Very few arms have yet been manufactured for the Government either at private or public establishments for a very obvious reason—there has not yet been time to get up establishments for this purpose. A few—eight or ten per day for four or five weeks past—it is reported, have been made out of gun-barrels saved from Harper's Ferry, at Wytheville, for the command of General Floyd. An order for 30,000 **stand** of arms has been given to Messrs. McElwain & Co., Holly Springs, Miss., the first delivery on which is to be made November 1, and thereafter at the rate of 2,000 per month. Mr. LeMat, of Louisiana, has an order to deliver 5,000 of his revolvers. Mr. Ed Want of New Berne, N. C., has an order for the delivery of 5,000 pistols, to begin in three months . . . Unlimited orders have also been given to parties to purchase arms in Mexico and Cuba. None have yet been received by this Department. The armory at this place (Richmond) will probably be in working order in six or eight weeks. That at Fayetteville, where some new buildings must be erected, will not be ready under four months. The Department has received from its agents in Europe for the purchase of arms, positive information as to the purchase by them of arms, embracing muskets and rifles chiefly, to the amount of $300,-000.00, and also assurances that they will be shipped through in safety. We therefore look forward with confidence to their early arrival."

South Carolina erected the State Military Works at Greenville in 1862 to repair and manufacture. Here were manufactured the Morse breech-loading weapons.

Most of the contracts whether by the Confederacy or by the individual states specified an arm of the description of either the Mississippi rifle or the Enfield rifle.

The Mississippi rifle was the U. S. model 1842, caliber 58, 33 acid-browned barrel with stud for sword bayonet. It earned its name from the Mississippi regiment that was armed with U. S. model 1842 and commanded by Jefferson Davis who though wounded and with a blood-filled boot rode his men to victory during the Mexican War. Adjutant General W. L. Sykes in January 1861 wrote:

"This arm being renowned for the brilliant victories achieved upon the battlefields of Mexico in the hands of the First Regiment of Mississippi Riflemen, has derived the appellation of Mississippi rifle, and is the principal arm called for by the volunteer corps."

The Enfield was Britain's Model 1855 rifled musket, caliber 577, 39" barrel, and adjustable rear sight brass guard and butt plate, 16" angular bayonet, iron bands.

Contracts for revolvers used either the Colt or the Whitney as their model.

As a subsidy to encourage firearm manufacture the Confederate government offered an advance of one third of the capital. This measure gave birth to some stillborn manufacturers with plans and a projected model and may explain the failure to find identifiable specimen of manufacturers mentioned in records, correspondence or contracts. Some of these pistol or revolver model or manufacturers are: Thomas W. Goodwin, Norfolk, Virginia; Felix Johnson, Florence, Alabama; E. J. Ligon, Demopolis, Alabama; Robinson & Lester, Richmond, Virginia; J. P. Sloat, Richmond, Virginia; Edward Want, Newberne, N. C., and Whitescarver, Campbell & Co., Rush, Texas.

Some of the state contracts were as follows:

These contracts were made with the Military Board of the State of Texas.

Billups & Hassell, Plentitude, Texas—700 rifles

Billups & Son, Plentitude, Texas—unspecified no. rifles

Short, Biscoe & Co., Tyler, Texas—5000 rifles

N. B. Tanner, Bastrop, Texas—500 rifles

Tucker, Sherrod & Co., Lancaster, Texas—3000 revolvers

Whitescarver, Campbell & Co., Rush, Texas—various quantities of rifles, 1,000 revolvers.

Alabama entered into the following contracts.

Davis & Bozeman, Coosa County, Ala.—882 Miss. rifles, 89 carbines delivered.

Dickson, Nelson & Co., Dawson, Ga.—645 Miss. rifles delivered.

Gray, John D., Graysville, Ga.—80 carbines delivered.

Gray, John M., Graysville, Ga.—96 Miss. rifles delivered.

Greenwood & Gray, Columbus, Ga.—253 Miss. rifles and 73 carbines delivered.

Kreutner, C.—36 Mississippi rifles delivered.

Sturdivant, Lewis G., Talladega—2000 rifles contract.

Suter, C. & Co. (P. Lessier)—50 Miss. rifles delivered.

Wallis, Daniel, Talladega, Ala.—1000 rifles contract.

Thus we have the five categories of Confederate firearms with class 1. Possession, class 2. Contribution, class 3. Purchase, class 4. Capture and class 5. Manufacture.

> *"No more shall the war cry sever,*
> *Or the winding rivers be red;*
> *They banish our anger forever*
> *When they laurel the graves of our dead*
> *Under the sod and the dew;*
> *Waiting the judgment day,*
> *Love and tears for the blue,*
> *Tears and love for the gray."*

CONFEDERATE GOVERNMENT ORDNANCE

T HESE NOTES were written by General Josiah Gorgas, chief of the ordnance department which he organized for the Confederate States and was responsible for its outstanding work.

Josiah Gorgas was born in Pennsylvania in 1818; a West Point graduate he was assigned to United States Army ordnance, served in the Mexican War and after the war in various arsenals. Stationed in Alabama (Mt. Vernon Arsenal) he married the daughter of ex-Governor Gayle in 1853. He later was transferred to Maine (Kennebec Arsenal), then to Charleston, South Carolina, and then to Pennsylvania. In April 1861 he resigned, returned to Alabama and was appointed by President Jefferson Davis as chief of ordnance.

The war over, Gorgas became superintendent of Briarfield Iron Works in Alabama; later headmaster and then vice-chancellor of the University of the South at Sewanee, Tennessee. In 1877 he became President of the University of Alabama. He died in 1883.

At the formation of the Government, or, at the beginning of the war, the arms at command were distributed as follows, as nearly as I can recollect:

Small Arms	Rifles	Muskets
At Richmond, Va. (about)	4,000	
Fayetteville Arsenal, North Carolina	2,000	25,000
Charleston Arsenal, South Carolina	2,000	20,000
Augusta Arsenal, Georgia	3,000	28,000
Mount Vernon Arsenal, Alabama	2,000	20,000
Baton Rouge Arsenal, Louisiana	2,000	27,000
	15,000	120,000

There were at Richmond about sixty thousand old, worthless flint muskets, and at Baton Rouge about ten thousand old Hall's rifles and carbines.

Besides the foregoing, there were at Little Rock,, Arkansas, a few thousand stands, and some few at the Texas Arsenals, increasing the aggregate of serviceable arms to, say, one hundred and forty-three thousand. To these must be added the arms owned by the several states and by military organizations throughout the country, giving, say, one hundred and fifty thousand in all for the use of the armies of the Confederacy. The rifles were of the caliber fifty-four, known as Mississippi rifles, except those at Richmond, taken from Harper's Ferry, which were caliber fifty-eight; the muskets were the old flintlock, caliber sixty-nine, altered to percussion. Of sabers there were a few boxes at each arsenal, and some short artillery swords. A few hundred holster pistols were scattered here and there. There were no revolvers.

AMMUNITION, POWDER AND LEAD

There was little ammunition of any kind, or powder, at the Arsenals in the South, and that little, relics of the Mexican War, stored principally at Baton Rouge and Mount Vernon Arsenals. I doubt whether there were a million rounds of small arm cartridges in the Confederacy. Lead there was none in store. Of powder the chief supply was that captured at Norfolk, though there was a small quantity at each of the Southern Arsenals, say sixty thousand pounds in all, chiefly old cannon powder. The stock of percussion caps could not have exceeded one quarter of a million.

ARTILLERY

There were no batteries of serviceable field artillery at any of the Southern Arsenals. A few old iron guns, mounted on Gribeaural carriages, fabricated about the time of the War of 1812, composed nearly the entire park, which the Confederate States fell heir to. There were some serviceable batteries belonging to the States, and some which belonged to volunteer companies. There were neither harness, saddles, bridles, blankets, nor other artillery or cavalry equipments.

Thus to furnish one hundred and fifty thousand men on both sides of the Mississippi, on, say, the 1st of May, 1861 there were on hand no infantry accounterments, no cavalry arms or equipments, no artillery, and, above all, no ammunition; nothing save small arms, and these almost wholly smooth-bore, altered from flint to percussion. Let us see what means we had for producing these supplies.

ARSENALS, WORKSHOPS, FOUNDARIES, ETC.

Within the limits of the Confederate States there were no arsenals at which any of the material of war was constructed. No arsenal, except that at Fayetteville, North Carolina, had a single machine above a foot-lathe. Such arsenals as there were had been used only as depots. All the work of preparation of material had been carried on at the North; not an arm, not a gun, not a gun-carriage, and, except during the Mexican War, scarcely a round of ammunition had for fifty years been prepared in the Confederate States. There were, consequently, no workmen, or very few of them, skilled in these arts. No powder, save perhaps, for blasting, had been made in the South; and there was no saltpeter in store at any point; it was stored wholly at the North. There was no lead, nor any mines of it, except on the northern limit of the Confederacy, in Virginia, and the situation of that made its product precarious. Only one cannon foundry existed—at Richmond. Copper, so necessary for field artillery and for percussion caps, was just being produced in East Tennessee. There was no rolling mill for bar iron south of Richmond, and but few blast furnaces, and these small and, with trifling exceptions, in the border States of Virginia and Tennessee. Such were the supplies and such the situation when I took charge of the Ordnance Department on the 8th of April 1861.

The first thing to be attended to was the supply of powder. Large orders had been sent to the North, both by the Confederate Government and some of the States, and these were being rapidly filled at the date of the attack on Fort Sumter. The entire product of one large Northern mill was being received at a Southern port. Of course, all the ports were soon sealed to such importations from the North. Attention was at once turned to the production of niter in North Alabama and in Tennessee—in the latter State under the energetic supervision of its Ordnance Department. An adequate supply of sulphur was found in New Orleans, where large quantities were in store to be used in sugar-refining. The entire stock was secured, amounting to some four or five hundred tons.

The erection of a large powdermill was early pressed by President Davis, and about the middle of June, 1861, he directed me to detail an officer to select a site and begin the work. The day after this order was given Colonel G. W. Rains, a graduate of West Point, in every way qualified for this service arrived in Richmond, through the blockade, and at once set out, under written instructions from me, to carry out the President's wishes. He, however, went first to East Tennessee to supervise and systematize the operations of two small private mills, which were then at work for the State of Tennessee.

Thus, in respect to powder and our means of making it, we had, perhaps, at this time (June 1, 1861), two hundred and fifty thousand pounds, chiefly cannon, at Norfolk and in Georgia, and as much more niter (mainly imported by the State of Georgia). We had no powdermills except the two crude ones just referred to, and no experience in making powder or in getting niter. All had to be learned.

As to a further supply of arms, steps had been taken by the president to import these and other ordnance stores from Europe; and Major Caleb Huse, a graduate of West Point, and at that moment professor in the University at Alabama, was selected to go abroad and secure them. He left Montgomery, under instructions, early in April, with credit of ten thousand pounds from Mr. Memminger. The appointment proved a happy one, for he succeeded with a very little money, in buying a good supply, and in running the Ordnance Department into debt for nearly a half million sterling—the very best proof of his fitness for his place, and of a financial ability which supplemented the narrowness of Mr. Memminger's purse.

Before this, and immediately upon the formation of the Confederate Government, Admiral Semmes had been sent to the North by President Davis as purchasing agent of arms and other ordnance stores, and succeeded in making contracts for, and purchases of powder, percussion caps, cap machinery (never delivered), revolvers, etc. He also procured drawings for a bullet-pressing machine and other valuable information.

The sets of machinery for making the rifle with sword bayonet, and the rifle-musket model of 1855, had been seized at Harper's Ferry by the State of Virginia. That for the rifle-musket was being transferred by the State to her ancient armory at Richmond under the direction of Lieutenant Colonel Burton, an officer in the service of Virginia, whose experience in the armories of the United States and in the erection of the works at Enfield, near London, qualified him above all for the work. The other set of machines was sent to Fayetteville, N. C., by consent of the State of Virginia, to be there re-erected, as there was at that point an arsenal with steam power and some good buildings, which had heretofore never been put to any use. These two sets of machinery—capable, it worked with but one set of hands to each, of producing two thousand to two thousand five hundred stands per month in all—were the only prospective resources at home. With additional workmen and some extension of the machinery, much larger results could be obtained. But the workmen were not to be had. As it was, it would take many months to put it in working order. Parts were missing and some injury done in the hasty transfer (partly under fire) from Harper's Ferry. There were no private armories at the South; nor was there any inducement, prior to the war, to turn capital in that direction. Thus, the class of skilled operatives needed were unknown to this region. In New Orleans the Brothers Cook were embarking in the business of making small arms, assisted by the purses and encouraged by the sympathy of patriotic citizens.

In field artillery the production was confined almost entirely to the Tredegar Works in Richmond. Some castings were made in New Orleans, and foundries were rapidly acquiring the necessary experience to produce good bronze castings. The Ordnance Department of Tennessee was also turning its attention to the manufacture of field and siege artillery at Nashville. At Rome, Georgia, a foundry—Noble & Son—was induced to undertake the casting of three-inch rifles after drawings furnished at Montgomery, but the progress made was necessarily slow. The State of Virginia possessed a number of old four pounder iron guns, which were reamed out to get a good bore, and were rifled with three grooves, after the manner of Parrott. The army in observation at Harper's Ferry and that at Manassas were supplied with old batteries of six-pounder guns and twelve-pounder howitzers. A few Parrott guns, purchased by the State of Virginia, were with Magruder at Big Bethel.

For the ammunition and equipments required for the infantry and artillery a good laboratory and shops had been established at Richmond by the State, but none of the Southern arsenals were yet in a condition to do much work. The arsenal at Augusta, Georgia, was directed to organize for the preparation of ammunition and the making of knapsacks, of which there were none wherewith to equip the troops now daily taking the field. The arsenal at Charleston and the depot at Savannah were occupied chiefly with local work. The arsenal at Baton Rouge was rapidly getting under way, and that at Mt. Vernon, Alabama, was also being prepared for work. None of them had facilities for the work usually done at an arsenal. Fayetteville, North Carolina, was in the hands of that State, and was occupied chiefly in repairing some arms and in making up a small amount of small arm ammunition. Little artillery ammunition was being made up, except for local purposes, save at Richmond.

Such was the general condition of supplies when the Government, quitting Montgomery, established itself at Richmond.

PROGRESS OF MANUFACTURE

Colonel Rains, in the course of the summer of 1861, established a refinery of saltpeter at or near Nashville, and to this point chiefly were sent the niter obtained from the State of Georgia, and that derived from caves in East and Middle Tennessee. He supplied the two powdermills in that with niter properly refined, and good powder was thus produced. A small portion of Georgia niter was sent to two small mills in South Carolina— at Pendleton and Walhalla—and a powder produced, inferior at first but afterward improved. The State of North Carolina established a mill near Raleigh, under contract with certain parties to whom the State was to furnish the niter, of which a great part was derived from caves in Georgia. A stamping mill was also put up near New Orleans, and powder produced before the fall of the city. Small quantities of powder were also received through the blockade from Wilmington to Galveston, some of it of very inferior quality. The great quantity of artillery placed in position from the Potomac to the Rio Grande required a vast supply of powder (there was no immediate want of projectiles) to furnish even the scant allowance of fifty rounds to each gun. I think we may safely estimate that on the 1st of January, 1862, there were fifteen hundred sea coast guns of various calibers in position from Evansport on the Potomac to Fort Brown on the Rio Grande. If we average their caliber at thirty-two pounders, and the charge at five jounds, it will, at forty rounds per gun, give us six hundred thousand pounds of powder for these. The field artillery, say three hundred guns, with two hundred rounds to the piece, would require, say one hundred and twenty-five thousand pounds and the small-arm cartridges, ten million, would consume one hundred and twenty-five thousand pounds more—making in all 850,000 pounds. If we deduct 250,000 pounds, supposed to be on hand in various shapes at the beginning of the war, we have as increment of 600,000 pounds. Of this perhaps 200,000 pounds had been made at the Tennessee and other mills, leaving 400,000 to have been supplied through the bockade and before the commencement of actual hostilities.

The site of the Government Powdermills was fixed at Augusta, Georgia on the report of Colonel Rains and progress was made on the work in this year. There were two large buildings, in the Norman (castellated) style of architecture; one contained the refinery and storeroom—the other being the mills, twelve in number. They were arranged in the best way on the canal which supplied water power to Augusta. This canal served as the means of transport for the material from point to point of its manufacture, though the mills were driven by steam. All the machinery, including the very heavy rollers, was made in the Confederate States. The various qualities of powder purchased, captured and produced were sources of irregularity in the ranges of our artillery and small arms—unavoidably so, of course. We were only too glad to take any sort of powder; and we bought some, brought into Florida, the best range of which scarcely exceeded one hundred and sixty yards with the eprouvette.

Contracts were made abroad for the delivery of niter through the blockade, and for producing it at home from caves. The amount of the latter delivered by contracts was considerable—chiefly in Tennessee.

The consumption of lead was in part met by the Virginia Lead Mines (Wytheville), the yield from which was 100,000 to 150,000 pounds per month. A laboratory for the smelting of other ores from the Silver Hill Mines, North Carolina and Jonesboro, East Tennessee, was put up at

Petersburg, under the direction of Dr. Piggott, of Baltimore. It was very well constructed; was capable of smelting a good many thousand pounds per day, and was in operation before mid-summer of 1862. Mines were opened on account of Government in East Tennessee, near the State Line of Virginia. They were never valuable, and were soon abandoned. Lead was collected in considerable quantities throughout the country by the laborious exertions of agents employed for this purpose. The battlefield of Bull Run was fully gleaned and much lead collected.

By the close of 1861 the following arsenals and depots were at work, having been supplied with some machinery and facilities, and were producing the various munitions and equipments required: Augusta, Georgia; Charleston, South Carolina; Fayetteville, North Carolina; Richmond, Virginia; Savannah, Georgia; Nashville, Tennessee; Memphis, Tennessee; Mount Vernon, Alabama; Baton Rouge, Louisiana; Montgomery, Alabama; Little Rock, Arkansas; and San Antonio, Texas—altogether eight arsenals and four depots. It would, of course, have been better, had it been practicable, to have condensed our work and to have fewer places of manufacture; but the country was deficient in the transportation which would have been required to place the raw material at a few arsenals. In this way only could we avail ourselves of local resources, both labor and material. Thus, by the close of 1861, a good deal had been done in the way of organization to produce the material of war needed by an army, as far as our means permitted. But our troops were still very poorly armed and equipped. The old smooth-bore musket was still the principal weapon of the infantry; the artillery had the six-pounder gun and twelve-pounder howitzer chiefly; and the cavalry were armed with anything they could get—sabers, horse pistols, revolvers, Hall's carbines (a wretched apology), sabers cut off, Sharp's carbines, musketoons, short Enfield rifles, etc. Equipments were, in many cases, made of stout domestic, stitched in triple folds and covered with paint or rubber, varnished.

But poor as were our arms, we had not enough of these to equip the troops which were pressing to the front in July and August, 1861. In the winter of 1861-62, while McClellan was preparing his great army near Alexandria, we resorted to the making of pikes for the infantry and lances for the cavalry; many thousands of the former were made at the various arsenals, but were little used. No access of enthusiasm could induce our people to rush to the field armed with pikes. I remember a formidable weapon, which was invented at this time, in the shape of a stout wooden sheath containing a two-edged straight sword some two feet long. The sheath or truncheon could be leveled, and the sword, liberated from the compression of a strong spring by touching a trigger, leaped out with sufficient force to transfix an opponent.

About December, 1861, arms began to come in through the purchases of Major Huse, and we had a good many Enfield rifles in the hands of our troops at Shiloh, which were received in time for use there through the blockade. Major Huse had found the market pretty well cleaned of arms by the late war in Europe, but he had succeeded in making contracts with private manufacturers, of which these arms were the result.

I will not attempt to trace the development of our work in its order, as I had first intended, but will note simply what I can recollect, paying some attention to the succession of events.

The winter of 1861-62 was the darkest period of my department. Powder was called for on every hand—Bragg at Pensacola, for his big ten-inch columbiads; Lovell, at New Orleans, for his extended defenses, and especially for his inadequate artillery at Fort Jackson and St. Phillips; Polk, at Columbus, Ky.; Johnston, for his numerous batteries on the Potomac; Magruder, at Yorktown. All these were deemed most important points. Then came Wilmington, Georgetown, Port Royal and Fernandia. Not a few of these places sent representatives to press their claims—Mr. Yulee, from Fernandia, and Colonel Gonzales, from Charleston. Heavy guns, too, were called for in all directions—the largest guns for smallest places.

The abandonment of the line of the Potomac and of the upper Mississippi, from Columbus to Memphis; the evacuation of the works below Pensacola and of Yorktown somewhat relieved us from the pressure for heavy artillery; and after the powder mills at Augusta went into operation in the fall of 1862, we had little trouble in supplying information.

To obtain the iron needed for cannon and projectiles, it became necessary to stimulate its production in Virginia, North Carolina, Tennessee, Georgia and Alabama. To this end, contracts were made with ironmasters in these States on liberal terms and advances of money made to them, to be refunded in products. These contracts were difficult to arrange, as so much had to be done for the contractor. He must have details from the army and the privilege of transport of provisions and other supplies over the railroads. And then the question of the currency was a continually recurring problem. Mr. Benjamin, who succeeded Mr. Walker in the War Department, gave me great assistance in the matter of making contracts, and seemed quite at home in arranging these details. His power of work was amazing to me, and he appeared as fresh at 12 o'clock at night, after a hard day's work, as he had been at 9 o'clock in the morning.

About May 1862, finding that the production of niter and of iron must be systematically pursued, and to this end thoroughly organized, I sought for the right person to place in charge of this vital duty. My choice fell on Colonel I. M. St. John (afterward Commissary General of Subsistence), and was eminently fortunate. He had the gift of organization, and I placed him in charge of the whole subject of producing niter from caves and from other sources, and of the formation of niter beds, which had already been begun in Richmond. Under his supervision beds were instituted at Columbia, South Carolina, Charleston, Savannah, Augusta, Mobile, Selma and various other points. We never extracted niter from these beds except for trial; but they were carefully attended to, enriched and extended, and were becoming quite valuable. At the close of 1864 we had, according to General St. John, 2,800,000 cubic feet of earth collected and in various stages of nitrification, of which a large proportion was prepared to yield one and a half pounds of niter per foot of earth, including all the niter beds from Richmond to Florida.

Through Colonel St. John, the whole niter-bearing area of the country was laid off into districts; each district in charge of an officer, who made his monthly reports to the office at Richmond. These officers procured details of workmen, generally from those subject to military duty in the mountain regions where disaffection existed, and carried on extended works in their several districts. In this way we brought up the niter production, in the course of a year, to something like half our total consumption of niter. It was a rude, wild sort of service; and the officers in charge of these districts, especially in East Tennessee, North Carolina and North Alabama, had to show much firmness in their dealings with the turbulent people among whom and by whose aid they worked. It is a curious fact that the district on which we could rely for the most constant yield of niter, having its headquarters at Greensboro, North Carolina, had no niter caves in it. The niter was produced by the lixiviation of nitrous earth dug from under old houses, barns, etc.

The niter production thus organized, there was added to the Niter Bureau the duty of supervising the production of iron, lead, copper, and, in fine, all the minerals which needed development, including the making of sulphuric and nitric acids; which later we had to manufacture to insure a supply of fulminate of mercury for our percussion caps. To give an idea of the extent of the duty thus performed: Colonel Morton, Chief of the Niter and Mining Bureau, after the transfer of General St. John, writes: "We were aiding and managing some twenty to thirty furnaces, with an annual yield of fifty thousand tons or more of pig metal. We had erected lead and copper smelting furnaces (at Petersburg, before referred to) with a capacity sufficient for all our wants, and had succeeded in smelting zinc of good quality at the same place." The chemical works were placed at Charlotte, North Carolina, where a pretty large leaden chamber for sulphuric acid was put up. Our chief supply of chemicals continued to come however from abroad, through the blockade, and these works, as well as our nitraries, were as much preparation against the day when the blockade might seal all foreign supply, as for present use. These constituted our reserves for final conflict.

We had not omitted to have a pretty thorough, though general, exploration of the mountain regions from Virginia to Alabama, with the hope of finding new deposits of lead. One of the earliest of these searches was made by Dr. Maupin, of the University of Virginia. No favorable results came from it. I remember an anecdote he told touching one of his researches. An old settler showed the doctor a small lump of lead which he had extracted from ore like some he had in his possession. There was the lead and here was the ore, but it was not an ore or lead. The doctor cross-examined: "Did he smelt it himself?" "Yes." "What in?" "An iron ladle." (Such as is used for running lead balls.) "Was there nothing in the ladle but this sort of ore?" "No, nothing." "Nothing at all? No addition— no flux?" "No, nothing but a little handful of common shot, thrown in to make it melt more easily."

Much of the niter region was close to the lines of the enemy, and here and there along its great extent became debatable ground. Not seldom the whole working force had to be suddenly withdrawn on the approach of the enemy, the "plant" hurried off, to be again returned and work resumed when the enemy had retired. Much of the work, too, lay in "Union" districts where our cause was unpopular and where obstacles of all kinds had to be encountered and overcome. It was no holiday duty, this niter digging, although the service was a good deal decried by such as knew nothing of its nature.

MANUFACTURE OF INFANTRY, ARTILLERY AND CAVALRY EQUIPMENTS

In equipping the armies first sent into the field the supply of these accessories was amazingly scant; and these deficiencies were felt more keenly, perhaps, than the more important want of arms. We had arms, such as they were, for over 100,000 men; but we had not accouterments nor equipments; and these had to be extemporized in a great measure. In time, knapsacks were little thought of by the troops, and we had at last contented ourselves with supplying haversacks, which the women (heaven reward their labors) could make, and for which we could get cotton cloth. But cartridge boxes we must have; and as leather was also needed for artillery harness and cavalry saddles, we had to divide the stock of leather the country could produce among these much-needed articles. But soldiers' shoes were even more needed than some of these; so that as all could not be fully provided, a scale of preference was established. Shoes and cartridge boxes were most needed, and then saddles and bridles. The President, whose practical sagacity was rarely at fault, early reduced these interests to logical sequence. He said, "For the infantry, men must first be fed, next armed, and even clothing must follow these; for if they are fed and have arms and ammunition they can fight." Thus the Subsistence Department had, in a general way, a preference for its requisitions on the Treasury; my department came next, and the Quartermaster's followed. Of course, the Medical Department had in some things the lead of all, for its duties referred to the men themselves, and it was necessary first of all to keep the hospitals empty and the ranks full.

To economize leather, the cartridge boxes and waist belts were made of prepared cotton cloth, stitched in three or four thicknesses. Bridle reins were also made, and even cartridge boxes covered with it, except the flap. Saddle skirts, too, were sometimes made in this way, heavily stitched. An ardent admirer of the South came over from Washington to offer his patent for making soldiers' shoes with no leather except the soles. The shoes were approved by all except those who wore them. The soldiers exchanged them with the first prostrate enemy who no longer needed his leathern articles. To get leather each department bargained for its own hides—made contracts with the tanner—procured hands for him by exemption from the army—got transportation over the railroads for the hides and for supplies and, finally, assisted the tanner to procure food for his hands and other supplies for his tannery. One can readily see from this instance how the labors of the heads of the departments became extended. Nothing but thorough organization could accomplish these multiplied and varied duties. We even established a fishery on the Cape Fear River to get oil for mechanical purposes, getting from the sturgeon beef at the same time for our workmen.

In cavalry equipments the main thing was to get a good saddle—one that did not ruin the back of the horse; for that, and not the rider's seat, is the point to be achieved. The rider soon accommodates himself to the seat provided for him. Not so the animal's back, which suffers from a bad saddle. We adopted Jenifer's tree, which did very well while the horses were in good condition, and was praised by that prince of cavalrymen, General J. E. B. Stuart; but it came down on the horse's backbone and withers as soon as the cushion of fat and muscle dwindled. The McClellan tree did better on the whole, and we finally succeeded in making a pretty good saddle of that kind—comfortable enough, but not as durable as the Federal article. In this branch of the service, one of the most difficult wants to supply was the horseshoe for cavalry and artillery. The want of iron and labor were both felt. Of course such a thing as a horseshoe machine, to turn out thousands an hour, was not to be dreamed of; besides, we would have had but little store of iron wherewith to feed it. Nor could we set up such machinery without much provision; for to concentrate all work on one machine required the transportation of iron to one point, and the distribution of the shoes from it to all the armies. But the railroads were greatly overtasked, and we were compelled to consider this point. Thus, we were led to employ every wayside blacksmith shop accessible, especially those in and near the theater of operations. These, again, had to be looked after, supplied with material, and exempted from service.

BUREAU OF FOREIGN SUPPLIES

It soon became obvious that in the Ordnance Department we must rely greatly on the introduction of articles of prime necessity through the blockade ports. As before stated, President Davis early saw this, and had an officer detailed to go abroad as the agent of the department. To systematize the introduction of the purchases, it was soon found advisable to own and run our own steamers. Major Huse made the suggestion also from that side of the water. Accordingly, he purchased and sent in the Robert E. Lee at a cost of $30,000, a vessel capable of stowing 650 bales of cotton. This vessel was kept running between Bermuda and Wilmington, and made some fifteen to eighteen successive trips before she was finally captured—the first twelve with the regularity of a packet. She was commanded first by Captain Wilkinson, of the Navy. Soon, the Cornubia, named the Lady Davis, was added, and ran as successfully as the R. E. Lee. She had a capacity of about 450 bales, and was, during the later part of her career, commanded also by a former naval officer, Captain R. H. Gayle. These vessels were long, low and rather narrow, built for swiftness and with their lights out and with fuel that made little smoke they contrived to slip in and out of Wilmington at pleasure, in spite of a cordon of Federal cruisers eager for the spoils of a blockade runner. Other vessels—the Eugenia, a beautiful ship, the Stag and several others—were added, all devoted to carrying ordnance supplies, and finally, general supplies. To supervise shipments at Bermuda, to which point they were brought by neutrals, either by steam or sail, Major Norman Walker was sent there by Mr. Secretary Randolph, about midsummer, 1862. Later, an army officer, Lieutenant Colonel Smith Stansbury, was detached to take charge of the stores accumulated there. Depots were likewise made at Nassau and Havana. Thus, much of the foreign organization.

But the organization of the business outside of our own soil was much the simplest part of the service. The home administration involved a variety of work so foreign to my other duties that I soon looked about for the proper person to discharge them in the most effective manner by exclusive devotion to them; and I had Lieutenant Colonel Bayne detailed to my office for this duty. He had been wounded at Shiloh, and on his recovery joined me about September, 1862.

It was soon found necessary, in order that the vessels coming in through the blockade might have their lading promptly on their arrival, that the bureau should undertake the procuring and shipment of cotton to Wilmington, Charleston and other points, for we had vessels arriving at half a dozen ports from Wilmington to Galveston. This necessitated the establishment of a steam compress at Wilmington, and, affiliated with it, agents to procure the cotton in the interior and see it to its destination; for the railroads were now so overtasked that it was only by placing positive orders from the Secretary of War in the hands of a selected agent that the cotton could be certainly forwarded over the various roads. The steam press was kept at work, in charge of Captain James M. Seixas (Washington Artillery). The necessity for transportation over the railroads brought us in contact with them, and gave them claim on us for assistance in the matter of supplies, such as steel, iron, copper, etc., and especially for work for various foundries and machine shops in which precedent was, of course, claimed for army work, and which were, therefore, in great part controlled by the Ordnance Department. The foreign supplies were not all conveyed through steamers. Contracts were out for supplies through Texas from Mexico.

Finding that the other departments of the Government would naturally claim a share in this avenue for supplies, which had been opened chiefly through my bureau, it was detached at my own insistence, but remained in charge of Colonel Bayne, with a good staff of officers and agents, as a separate bureau.

Thus, the Ordnance Department consisted of a Bureau proper of Ordnance, having its officers in the field and at the arsenals and depots; of the Niter and Mining Bureau, and of the Bureau of Foreign Supplies.

DEVELOPMENT OF THE ARSENALS, ARMORIES AND OTHER PLACES OF MANUFACTURE OF ORDANCE STORES

The arsenal at Richmond soon grew into very large dimensions, and produced all the ordnance stores that an army may require, except cannon and small arms in quantities sufficient to supply the forces in that part of the field. I have, by accident, preserved a copy of the last number of the Richmond Enquirer, published under Confederate rule. It is dated April 1, 1865, and contains the following: "Statement of the principal issues from the Richmond Arsenal from July 1, 1861, to January 1, 1865":

"341 columbiads and siege guns (these were made at the Tredegar Works, but issued from the arsenal); 1,306 field pieces made chiefly at Tredegar works or captured; 1,375 gun carriages; 875 Caissons; 152 forges; 6,852 sets of artillery harness; 921,441 rounds field, siege and seacoast ammunition; 1,456,190 friction primers; 1,110,966 fuses; 17,423 port fires; 3,985 rockets; 323,231 infantry arms (most of these were turned in from the army, from battlefields and from the Richmond Armory); 34,067 cavalry arms (same remark); 44,877 swords and sabers (from army, battlefield and contractors); 375,510 sets of infantry and cavalry accouterments; 180,181 knapsacks; 328,977 canteens and straps; 72,413,854 small-arm cartridges; 115,087 gun and carbine slings; 146,901,250 percussion caps; 69,418 cavalry saddles; 85,139 cavalry bridles; 75,611 cavalry halters; 35,464 saddle blankets; 59,624 pairs spurs; 42,285 horse brushes; 56,903 curry combs."

This "statement" appears as an editorial, but the items were furnished from the office of the arsenal, and may be relied on. Its commandant at this time was Lieutenant Colonel Leroy Broun, of Virginia. In the items of cavalry saddles, bridles, harness, infantry accouterments, canteens and other articles of this character, much assistance was received from contractors. A small part of the percussion caps also came from other arsenals. When we reflect that the arsenal grew to these great dimensions in a little over two years, it must be confessed that good use was made of the time. The laboratory attached to the arsenal was well conducted and did much work. It covered the island known as Green Island, which was connected with the shore by a bridge built by the Engineer Department especially for the service of this laboratory.

Besides the cap machinery, which was a very large and improved plant, machinery for pressing balls, for driving time fuses, for drawing friction primers and metallic cartridges and other labor-saving machines were invented, made and used with effect. In all respects the establishment, though extemporized and lodged in a cluster of tobacco warehouses, was equal to the first class arsenals of the United States in extent and facilities.

The arsenal of Augusta, Georgia, was in great part organized in the city, where suitable buildings were obtained, and did much the same class of work done at Richmond, though on a smaller scale. It was very serviceable to the armies serving in the South and West, and turned out a good deal of field artillery complete, the castings being excellent. Colonel George W. Rains, in charge of the arsenal and powder works, found that the fusion of a small percent of iron with the copper and tin improved the strength of the bronze castings very much.

The powder mills at Augusta, Georgia, which I have already mentioned as the direct result of the order of President Davis, were wonderfully successful and never met with serious accident—a safe indication of the goodness of its arrangements. It showed, too, that, under able directions, the resources of Southern workshops and the skill of its artisans had already become equal to the execution of great enterprises involving high mechanical skill.

The arsenal and workshops at Charleston were also enlarged, steam introduced, and good work done in various departments.

The arsenal at Mount Vernon, now furnished with steam power and having a good deal of machinery, was considered out of position after the fall of New Orleans, and was moved to Selma, Alabama, where it grew into a large well-ordered arsenal of the best class, under the charge of

Lieutenant Colonel White. It was relied on to a great extent for the equipment of the troops and fortifications in the southern part of the Confederacy.

Attracted by the deposits of fine ore immediately north of Selma, made accessible by the Selma, Rome and Dalton Railroad, the War Department accepted the proposition of Mr. Colin McRae to undertake the erection at Selma of a large foundry for the casting of cannon of the heaviest caliber. A large contract was made with him and advances of money made from time to time as the work progressed. After a time Mr. McRae was called on by President Davis to go abroad in connection with Confederate finances. He made it a condition that he should be relieved of his works and contract at Selma without pecuniary loss to himself. The works were thereupon assumed by the War and Navy Departments jointly, and placed at first under the charge of Colonel Rains as general superintendent, while an officer of less rank took immediate charge. Subsequently, it was agreed by the War Department that the Navy should take sole charge, and use the works for its own purposes. It was here that Commander Brooke made many of his formidable banded and rifled guns.

The foundry and rolling mills grew into large proportions, supplied by the iron and coal of that region. Had the Confederacy survived, Selma bid fair to become the Pittsburgh of the South. The iron obtained from the brown haematite at the furnaces in Bibb County (Brierfield), and from the Shelby works, was admirable, the former being of unusual strength.

Mount Vernon arsenal was still continued, after being in a great measure dismantled, and was utilized to get lumber and timber for use elsewhere, and to gather and prepare moss for making saddle blankets.

At Montgomery, shops were kept up for the repair of small arms, and for the manufacture of articles of leather, of which some supplies were obtained in that region.

There were many other small establishments and depots, some of them connected immediately with the army, as at Dublin, Southwest, Virginia; Knoxville, Tennessee; and Jackson, Mississippi. Some shops at Lynchburg, Virginia, were moved to Danville, near the south line of Virginia, and it grew into place of some value for repairs, etc.

The ordnance shops at Nashville had been hurriedly transferred to Atlanta, Georgia, on the fall of Fort Donelson; and when Atlanta was seriously threatened by the operations of Sherman, the arsenal there, which had become very important, was moved to Columbus, Georgia, where there was the nucleus of an ordnance establishment. Colonel M. H. Wright soon made this nearly as valuable as his arsenal at Atlanta had been.

ARMORIES AND SMALL ARMS

Besides the arsenals, a brief account of which has just been given, we had the armories at Richmond and Fayetteville, North Carolina, and arms were also made at other points.

The state of Virginia claimed all machinery captured at Harper's Ferry, and was bringing it all to Richmond. It was agreed, however, with the state of North Carolina, that that part of the machinery which was specially adopted to make the Mississippi rifle (caliber 54) should go to Fayetteville, where there was an arsenal with good steam power, the machinery to be returned at the close of the war to the state of Virginia. Colonel Burton, an admirably educated machinist, superintended the re-erection of the works at Richmond. He was subsequently made Superintendent of Armories, and given full charge of the entire subject of manufacture of arms in the Confederacy. The machinery of the rifle—musket (caliber 58), retained at Richmond, got to work as early as September, 1861. If we had possessed the necessary number of workmen this "plant" could have been so filled in as to have esily produced 5,000 stands per month, working night and day. As it was, I don't think it ever turned out more than 1,500 in any one month. Fayetteville did not get to work until the spring of 1862 and did not average 400 per month, for want of hands.

To supplement this scarcity of operatives, Colonel Huse was authorized to engage for us a number of skilled workmen, used to work on small arms, and to pay their passage over. They came in through the blockade at Wilmington without difficulty, but we could do nothing with them. They had been engaged to be paid in gold, which in the meantime had risen to such a price as to make their pay enormous, and would have produced utter disintegration among our own operatives. I offered to pay one half of the wages promised them in gold, to their families in England, if they would take the remainder in Confederate money, which would support them here. I brought the British Consul to confer with them here. But they stood upon their bond; and foreseeing that their presence would do more harm than good, I simply, with their consent, reshipped them by the next steamer, and paid their passage back. The experiment cost us something like 2,000 in gold, and made us shy of foreign workmen, especially English. I think the Treasury Department did succeed in getting engravers and printers for their purposes at Columbia, South Carolina, to some extent by importation; but my impression is they were not English. Of all obstinate animals I have ever come in contact with, these English workmen were the most unreasonable.

The Cook Brothers had, as heretofore stated, undertaken the making of rifle-muskets in New Orleans at the very commencement of the war. On the fall of New Orleans their machinery was hurriedly taken off by boats up the Mississippi. They finally selected Athens, Georgia, as their point of manufacture, and under a contract with me, and assisted with funds under that contract, proceeded to reorganize and extend their "plant." They were reasonably successful.

The want of cavalry arms caused me to make a contract with parties in Richmond to make the Sharp's carbine—at that time the best cavalry arm we had. A set of machinery capable of turning out one hundred arms a day was driven to completion in less than a year, nearly all the machinery being built up "from the stumps." The arms were nearly perfect, chiefly for want of nice workmanship about the "cut-off." It was not gas-tight. We soon bought out the establishment, and converted it into a manufactory of rifle-carbines, caliber 58, as the best arm our skill would enable us to supply to the cavalry.

Recognizing the **necessity of some great central establishment for the** production of small arms, plans of buildings and estimates of machinery were made for such a one, to be built at Macon, Georgia,—a point of easy access and near to a fertile corn region out of the way of the enemy. Colonel Burton went to England and easily negotiated for the machinery, which was to have been of sufficient capacity to turn out about ten thousand arms per month. Buildings were immediately obtained for some machinery for pistols, which was transferred there; and Colonel Burton had made good progress in erecting ample buildings for the new machinery, part of which had arrived at Bermuda and Nassau when the Confederacy fell. But about six months before the close of the war, finding that the blockade had become so stringent that the introduction of machinery would be very difficult, and reflecting, too, that as long as the war continued, this extended machinery would be of but little use to us, for want of workmen, I got the authority of the Secretary of War to set it up at some point abroad and bring in the arms, which would be less difficult than to bring in the machinery and train the workmen. Colonel Burton was abroad on this duty when the war closed. Had the war been prolonged, we should, in twelve months, have been making our own arms in a foreign land, under the sanction of a private name. After the war it was proposed to transfer the entire "plant" to the buildings which were in course of construction for it at Macon. Peace would have then found us in possession of a great armory, which I much desired.

One of the earliest difficulties forced upon us in the manufacture of arms was to find an iron fit for the barrels. The "skelps" found a Harper's Ferry served for awhile, and when these were exhausted, Colonel Burton selected an iron produced at a forge in Patrick County, Virginia, and by placing a skilled workman over the rolling process at the Tredegar Works, he soon produced "skelps" with which he was satisfied. We found that almost any of the good brown haematite ores produced an iron of ample strength for the purpose, and the even grain and toughness could be attained by careful rerolling.

Besides the larger armories at Richmond and Fayetteville, smaller establishments grew up at Asheville, North Carolina, and at Tallassee, Alabama. The former was the development of a private enterprise undertaken to repair and fit up old arms, by a citizen (Mr. Pullem) resident there, and afterward as a matter of necessity, assumed by the Confederate Government. Most of the machinery was moved before the close of the war to Columbia, South Carolina, whither, as a place of safety, other arms manufacturing machinery was moved from other points. Tallassee was selected as a good manufacturing point, a large building having been offered to us by the proprietors of the cotton mills there, and some machinery for making pistols moved thither from Columbus, Georgia.

A great part of the work of our armories consisted in repairing arms brought in from the battlefield or sent in from the armies in too damaged a condition to be effectually repaired at the arsenals. In this way only could we utilize all the gleanings of the battlefields. My recollection is that we saved nearly ten thousand stands of arms from the field of Bull Run, and that the battlefields about Richmond in 1862 gave us about 25,000 excellent arms through the labors of the Armory at Richmond.

The original stock of arms, it will be remembered, consisted almost wholly of smooth-bore muskets, altered from flint to percussion, using ounce balls (caliber 69). There were some 15,000 to 20,000 Mississippi rifles; and then some irregular arms, like Hall's rifles and carbines—some short carbines smooth-bore; and there were even some of the old flintlock muskets. All this original stock disappeared almost wholly from our armies in the first two years of the war, and were replaced by a better class of arms, rifled and percussioned. It is pretty safe to assume that we had altogether, east and west of the Mississippi, 300,000 infantry, pretty well armed, by the middle of 1863. We must therefore have procured at least that number for our troops. But we must also have supplied the inevitable waste of two years of active warfare. Placing the good arms thus lost at the moderate estimate of 100,000, we must have received from various sources 400,000 stands of infantry arms in the two years of fighting ending July 1, 1863. I can only estimate from memory the several sources from which this supply was derived as follows:

Good rifled arms on hand at the beginning of the war (this includes the arms in the hands of volunteer companies)	25,000
New arms manufactured in the Confederacy and in private establishments	40,000
Arms received from the battlefields and put in good order (this includes the great number of arms picked up by the soldiers)	150,000
Imported from January 1, 1862 to July 1, 1863	185,000
Total	400,000

This estimate does not include pistols and sabers, of which a small supply was imported.

To account for the very large number obtained from the enemy (rather an under than an over estimate), it must be remembered that in some fights, where our troops were not finally successful, they were so at first, and swept over the camps and positions of the enemy. Whenever a Confederate soldier saw a weapon better than his own he took it and left his inferior arm; and although he may have been finally driven back, he kept his improved musket. So, too, on every field there were partial successes, which in the early part of the war resulted in improved weapons; and although on another part of the field there may have been a reverse, the enemy had not the same advantage; the Confederate arms being generally inferior to those of the adversaries. The difference of arms was not so marked at a later day, except in cavalry arms, in which we were always at a disadvantage, the celebrated Spencer carbine being generally in the hands of the enemy's cavalry during the last two years of the war.

A CENTRAL LABORATORY

The unavoidable variation in the ammunition made at the different arsenals, pointed out, early in the war, that there should be a general superintendent of all the laboratories, invested with authority to inspect and supervise their manipulations and materials. To this end Lieutenant Colonel Mallet, a chemist and scientist of distinction, who had for some years been professor in the University of Alabama, was selected and placed in charge of this delicate and important duty. I attribute much of the improvement in our ammunition to this happy selection. A more earnest and capable officer I cannot imagine. What a set of men we would have had after the war out of which to form an ordnance department, had we been successful. Raisn, St. John, Mallet, Burton, Wright, White, Baldwin, Rhett, Ellicott, Andrews, Childs, DeLagnel, Hutter and others who would have remained in the service. Then there were some no less admirable, like LeRoy Brown, Allan, Wiley Browne, Morton, Colston, Bayne, Cuyler, E. B. Smith, etc., who would doubtless have returned to their civil avocations.

Among the obvious necessities of a well-regulated service was one large central laboratory, where all ammunition should be made—thus securing absolute uniformity where uniformity was vital. The policy of dissemination so necessary to husband our transportation and to utilize the labor of non-combatants must here yield to the greater necessity of obtaining our ammunition uniform in quality and in dimensions. Authority was, therefore, obtained from the War Department to concentrate this species of work at some central laboratory. Macon, Georgia was selected, and Colonel Mallet placed in charge of the central laboratory, as Burton was later placed in charge of a national armory. Plans of the buildings and of the machinery required were submitted to the Secretary of War, approved, and the work begun with energy. This pile of buildings had a facade of 600 feet, was designed with taste, and comprehended every possible appliance for good and well-organized work. The buildings were nearly ready for occupation at the close of the war, and some of the machinery had arrived at Bermuda. In point of time, this project preceded that of the National Armory, and was much nearer completion. These, with our admirable powder mills at Augusta, would have completed a set of works for the Ordnance Department; and in them we would have been in condition to supply arms and munitions to 300,000 men. To these would have been added a foundry for heavy guns at Selma or Brierfield, Alabama, at which later place the strongest cast iron in the country was produced, and where we had already purchased and were carrying on a furnace for the production of cold-blast charcoal pig for this special purpose. All these establishments were in the heart of the country not readily reached by the enemy, and were, in fact, never reached by them until just at the close of the war. Being in or near an excellent agricultural region, they would have had the advantage of cheap living for operatives; and they had all sufficient facilities for transportation, being situated on main lines of railroads.

SUMMARY

I have thus, from memory, faintly traced the development of the means and resources by which our large armies were supplied with arms and ammunition. This involved manufacturing, mining and importation. The last two were confided in time to sub-bureaus created ex necessitate, which were subsequently detached. The first was carried on by the armories, arsenals, laboratories and depots above mentioned. We began in April, 1861, without an arsenal, laboratory or powermill of any capacity, and with no foundry or rolling mill, except at Richmond, and before the close of 1863, in little over two years, we had built up, during all the harassments of war, holding our own in the field defiantly and successfully against a powerful and determined enemy. Crippled as we were by a depreciated currency; throttled with a blockade that deprived us of nearly all means of getting material or workmen; obliged to send almost every able-bodied man to the field; unable to use the slave labor with which we were abundantly supplied, except in the most unskilled departments of production; hampered by want of transportation even of the commonest supplies of food; with no stock on hand even of the articles, such as steel, copper, lead, iron, leather, which we must have to build up our establishments; and in spite of these deficiencies we persevered at home as determinedly as did our troops in the field against a more tangible opposition, and in a little over two years created, almost literally out of the ground, foundries and rolling mills (at Selma, Richmond, Atlanta and Macon); smelting works (at Petersburg), chemical works (at Charlotte, North Carolina), a powdermill far superior to any in the United States and unsurpassed by any across the ocean, and a chain of arsenals, armories and laboratories equal in their capacity and their improved appointments to the best of those in the United States, stretching link by link from Virginia to Alabama. Our people were justly proud of the valor and constancy of the troops which bore their banners bravely in the front of the enemy; but they will also reflect that these creations of skill and labor were the monuments which represented the patience, industry and perseverence of the devoted and patriotic citizens; for of the success which attended the operations of any department of the Confederate Government, the larger moiety was due to the cooperation of the body of the people—a cooperation founded in their hearty sympathy with and their entire faith in the cause which that government represented.

ORGANIZATION

The Ordnance Bureau, as finally organized, consisted of one brigadier general, one colonel, and of such additional number of field officers, captains and first lieutenants as the service required. They were artillery officers on ordnance duty.

Appointments to these positions were at first made by selections, on nomination by the Ordnance Bureau, but about October, 1862, Congress created fifty officers of artillery especially for ordnance duty, to which two hundred more were subsequently added. As selection for these officers involved much political contrivance, I obtained the order of the Secretary of War to hold examinations for appointment to the grade of captain and first lieutenant. This plan succeeded entirely and relieved us from a thousand personal solicitations. The first examination was held at Richmond. Of some five hundred applications found on file for ordnance officers, less than one hundred came to the examination, and of these only some forty or fifty passed. The examination for captain involved a fair knowledge of a college course of mathematics, and none, I believe, passed this except the M.A.s of the University of Virginia. That for the first lieutenant embraced only an ordinary English education, with a full examination on the Ordnance Manual. This gave us an excellent set of officers—educated men; and although a few of them were, as it was said, "Virginia schoolmasters," and cannot be said to have distinguished themselves professionally, yet they were all respectable on account of their education, and I am sure there never were in any respect a better class of such officers.

These examinations were extended, and were held at the headquarters of each army in the field by a commission, of which Lieutenant Colonel Leroy Broun and Lieutenant Colonel S. Stansbury, Colonel T. A. Rhett and Major J. Wilcox Browne were the chief members. These, or one of them, went to an army and associated with themselves one or more officers detailed by the general at headquarters. In order to provide for that class of valuable officers, distinguished for excellent qualities developed by service on the field but not prepared for a somewhat technical examination, each general of an army designated one or two of his class, who were appointed on his recommendation alone.

Officers in the field were distributed as follows: To each army a "chief ordnance officer," with the rank of lieutenant colonel; to each army corps, an ordnance officer with the rank of major; to each division, a captain, and to each brigade a first lieutenant; all these attached to the staff of their respective generals, but reporting also directly, if necessary, to the ordnance officer, through his superior in the field, and receiving instructions as to special duties through the same channel. Every regiment had an ordnance sergeant in charge of ordnance wagon, containing the spare arms and the ammunition of each regiment.

The officers in command of the greater ordnance establishments—such as Richmond and Augusta, etc.,—had the grade of lieutenant colonel, like the "chief ordnance officers" of armies in the field, while in the lesser establishments the officers had rank according to the gravity of the duties devolving on them.

The Superintendent of Armories, Lieutenant Colonel Burton, and the Superintendent of Laboratories, Lieutenant Colonel Mallet, had also the grade of the higher officers on duty in the field.

The labor and responsibilities of my department closed practically at Charlotte, North Carolina, on the 26th of April, when the President left that place with an escort for the Trans-Mississippi. My last stated official duty, that I can recall, was to examine a cadet in the Confederate service for promotion to commissioned officer.

On the afternoon of the 25th of April I received due formal notice from the Adjutant General's office that General Lawton, Quartermaster General, General Gilmer, Chief Engineer, and I were constituted a Board of Examiners on Cadet _____. We met a little before sundown, in the ample upper story of a warehouse in Charlotte, North Carolina, and by the waning light of the last day of the Confederate Government, we went through all the stages of an examination of an expectant lieutenant of the Confederate armies. Lawton, I think, took him on geography and history, Gilmer on the mathematics, while I probably tested his English grammar. He passed the ordeal in triumph and got his commission, which I daresay he prizes very highly, as he ought to do, considering the august body that signed the certificate which pronounced him qualified for it.

DETACHED OBSERVATION

Consumption of Small Arms Cartridges

It appears that the Richmond laboratory made seventy-two million cartridges in three and a half years, say one thousand working days. As this laboratory made nearly as much as all the others combined, we may safely place the entire production at one hundred and fifty million, or 150,000 per day. As our reserves remained nearly the same, being but slightly increased toward the latter part of the war, there must have been only a little less than this consumption in the field, say half a cartridge per man per day for the average force of 300,000 men, to cover all the accidents and expenditures of service in the field. An average, then, of half a cartridge per day per man would be a safe assumption for protracted warfare.

In examining the returns of ordnance officers after heavy actions, I found that the reduction of ammunition amounted to from about nineteen to twenty-six rounds per man. At Gettysburg the reports of a few days before the battle and a short time after showed a difference of twenty-five or twenty-six rounds on the average. This was the heaviest consumption to which my attention was called. When our troops first took the field commanders were very nervous because they had only fifty to seventy rounds per man instead of the two hundred rounds prescribed by the Ordnance Manual. Later, we raised it to about eighty or ninety rounds. The results of battles show that with proper dispositions for transfer from one corps to another, there need be no scarcity with sixty rounds on hand, or even fifty.

Our soldiers were, however, in the habit of supplying themselves with ammunition by throwing away their empty cartridge boxes and taking any well-supplied one that they might espy with the proper cartridges. What splendid fellows they were, taking even better care of their powder and lead than of themselves, or of their rations. They were in downright earnest.

Consumption and Supply of Lead

Allowing for waste, 150,000,000 of cartridges would require ten million pounds of lead for these alone, to say nothing of other needs. Where did all this lead come from? I make the following rough calculation:

	Pounds
From Trans-Mississippi mines (early in the war)	400,000
From the mines in Virginia (60,000 lbs. per month)	2,160,000
On hand at arsenals, etc.	140,000
Imported (not over)	2,000,000
Picked up through the country and on battlefields	5,300,000
Total	10,000,000

This leads to the surprising conclusion that we must have picked up throughout the country over 5,300,000 pounds of lead during the four years of the war. I remember that the window weights and loose lead about the house yielded 200,000 pounds in Charleston alone; while the disabused lead water pipes in Mobile supplied, if I am not mistaken, as much more, so that these two items alone supplied one thirteenth of this vast gleaning of the country.

Transfer of Arms to the South

It was a charge often repeated against Governor Floyd that, as Secretary of War, he had, with traitorous intent, abused his office by sending arms to the South just before the secession of the States. The transactions which gave rise to this accusation were in the ordinary course of an economical administration of the War Department. After it had been determined to change the old flintlock musket, which the United States possessed, to percussion, it was deemed cheaper to bring all the flintlock arms in store at Southern arsenals, to the Northern arsenals and armories for alteration, rather than to send the necessary machinery and workmen to the South. Consequently, the Southern arsenals were stripped of their deposits, which were sent to Springfield, Watervliet, Pittsburgh, St. Louis, Frankford, Penn., and other points. After the conversion had been completed the denuded Southern arsenals were again supplied with about the same numbers, perhaps slightly augmented, that had formerly been stored there. The quota deposited at the Charleston Arsenal, where I was stationed in 1860, arrived there fully a year before the opening of the war.

The Napoleon Field-guns

I think I will be sustained by the artillery in saying that, on the whole, this gun became the favorite for field service, perhaps because our rifle shells with percussion fuses were, as stated by General Alexander, less successful than that of the enemy. When copper became scarce, we fabricated an iron Napoleon with a wrought iron jacket, weighing in all twelve hundred and fifty pounds, which was entirely satisfactory, and was cheerfuly accorded by the artillery companionship with their bronze favorites. The simplicity and certainty of the ammunition of this smooth-bore, its capacity for grape and canister, its good range, and its moderate draught, as it was not too heavy for four horses, were certainly strong reasons in its favor. At the distance at which the serious work of the artillery was done, it was an overmatch for rifled artillery.

Heavy Guns

It was, of course, a matter of keen regret to me that we could not rapidly produce guns of heavy caliber for points; the defense of which against men-of-war, was of vital importance. But the ten-inch columbiad could only be cast at the Tredegar Works, and although this establishment was in able hands and responded nobly to the calls made upon it, yet tasked, as it was, to produce artillery of all calibers—especially field artillery—we could but slowly answer the appeals made with equal vehemence from Pensacola, Yorktown, Charleston and New Orleans.

About the close of 1863, Major Huse sent two Blakely rifles of about thirteen-inch caliber, splendid looking, superbly mounted, and of fearful cost!— $10,000 for two in England, with fifty rounds each. Charleston claimed them on their arrival at Wilmington, and I was glad to strengthen General Beauregard's hands. Unfortunately, one of them cracked in some trial firing, with comparatively weak charges. The full charge, which was never reached, was fifty pounds of powder, and a solid rifle shell of say 450 pounds. These guns were built up of a wrought-iron cylinder, closed at the breech with a brass-screw plug, some thirty inches long, and chambered to seven inches. This cylinder had three successive jackets, each shorter than its predecessor, so that from muzzle to breech the thickness of the gun increased by steps of about three and a half inches. The object of the seven-inch chamber in the brass plug was to afford an air or gas space which would diminish the strain on the gun. Such was the theory. General Ripley, however, cut down the big cartridge bags of ten or eleven inches in diameter, so as to introduce the charge into the brass chamber. This not being over three inches thick, cracked and the crack, I believe, extended into the cylinder. On a report of the facts direct from Charleston to Captain Blakely, he attributed the bursting to the high elevation given, though the highest, I think, had been only about one hundred and fifty; an impotent conclusion for a scientific artillerist to reach. The fact of the introduction of the charge into the air space may have been omitted in the narrative to him, and thus he may have been drawn into this helpless conclusion. I never saw the drawings of the gun until after the report of the accident. Captain Brooke, Chief of Ordnance of the Navy, with me then looked over the drawings and evolved the design of the air chamber. After this the gun was fired, and with moderate elevations attained fair but not remarkable ranges, as I was advised. The cracked gun was skillfully repaired at Charleston, and restored to a reliable condition.

Just before the war closed, the Tredegar works had cast its first twelve-inch gun, after the method of Rodman—cast on a hollow core, with water kept flowing in and out of it to cool the castings from the inside. This method of cooling has been found to give a marked increase of strength, and greater hardness and consequent smoothness to the finished bore.

ASHEVILLE RIFLE
Asheville, N. C.

Firm consisted of Robert William Pulliam, Ephriam Clayton and G. W. Whitson. Modified Enfield, 58 Cal., 32⅝″ bbl., brass mountings, lock plate m. "Asheville, N. C."

AUSTRIAN RIFLE
Tyler, Texas

Cal., 55; bbl., 37¼″; iron mounting; 2 bands, 2 sling swivels. Lockplate (forward of hammer). "Austrian Rifle, Tyler, Tex. Cal. 54″ (rear of hammer) "C.S. year."

BAKER RIFLE
Fayetteville, N. C.

Cal. 52, bbl. 36″, U.S. Model 1817, converted from flintlock to perc. Lockplate m. "M. A. Baker, Fayetteville, N. C." bbl. m. "N. Carolina"

BILLUPS RIFLE
Mound Prairie, Texas

Mfgd. about 1,000 rifles, possible Miss. rifle description. Contract in 1862 to Billups & Hassell, partnership of John D. Billups and Daniel D. Hassell. Hassell died and contract assumed by Billups and Son, a partnership of Joseph D. Billups and his son, Joseph Billups.

C. S. & P. RISING-BREECH CARBINE

Cal. 54; 21″ bbl. Bbl. and breech-block marked "C.S. & P." Percussion breech-loader; pull down the trigger guard and the breech-block rises vertically.

COOK & BROTHER ARTILLERY RIFLE

(F. W. C. Cook and Francis L. Cook)

New Orleans and in 1862 removed to Athens, Georgia. Excellent workmanship.

Cal. 58; bbl. 24"; all brass mountings. Lockplate (front of hammer)—"Cook & Brother, Athens, Ga. year plus serial number. (Rear of hammer)—Confederate flag. Butt plate has serial number; Bbl. m. "Athens—year—proved."

COOK & BROTHER INFANTRY RIFLE

Close copy Enfield. Cal. 58; bbl. 33". Brass mountings, iron ramroad with brass cup-shaped end; butt plate has serial number; bbl. has serial no. plus year. Lockplate (front of hammer) "Cook & Brother, Athens, Ga." Year —serial number. (rear of hammer) Confederate flag.

COOK & BROTHER MUSKETOON

Cal. 58; bbl. 21". Brass mountings; swivel ramrod with large button head end; clamping bands. Lockplate (front of hammer) "Cook & Brother, Athens, Ga.; year & serial number. (rear of hammer) Confederate flag. Serial number marked on breech of barrel and butt plate.

DAVIS & BOZEMAN RIFLE

Central, Alabama

Cal. 59, bbl. 33", lockplate m. "D. & B. Ala. 1864" breech m. "Ala. 1864."

DICKSON, NELSON & CO. CARBINE

William Dickson, Dickson, Ala.; O. O. Nelson, Tuscumbia, Ala; L. H. Sadler, Leighton, Ala. organized Shakanoosa Arms Co. and received contract from State of Alabama for rifles. Began to build plant at Dickson, Ala., but war changes compelled them to move to Rome, Ga.; a fire destroyed the building and they moved to Adairsville, Ga.; war changes compelled them to move to Dawson, Ga.; and in Georgia the arms were manufactured with Alabama markings.

Cal. 58; bbl 24"; lockplate (forward of hammer) "Dickson, Nelson & Co.

C.S." (rear of hammer) "Ala. & year."

DICKSON, NELSON & CO. RIFLE

Close copy U. S. model 1855; lock of U. S. model 1842 Cal. 58—bbl. 33"; brass mountings, 2 leaf rear sight. Lockplate (front of hammer) "Dickson, Nelson & Co. C.S." (rear of hammer) "Ala. & year"; bbl. m. "Ala. 1863"; butt plate m. "Ala."

FAYETTEVILLE ARMORY RIFLE

Fayetteville, N. C.

Used machinery removed from Harper's Ferry.

Cal. 58, bbl. 33"; two bands, brass buttplate m. "C.S.A." lockplate, "Fayetteville, eagle with outspread wings, C.S.A., year." Note: S in C.S.A. is inverted.

GEORGIA ARMORY RIFLE

Milledgeville State Penitentiary, Ga.

Cal. 58, bbl. 33", brass butt plate, trigger guard; lockplate (all in rear of hammer) "Ga. Armory & year."

LAMB RIFLE

Jamestown, N. C.

Lamb & Brother also H. C. Lamb & Company.

Cal. 58, bbl. 33" (7" at breech octagon, 26" round): yellow oak stock stamped, "H. C. Lamb & Co., N. C." plus serial number; serial no. also on breech and inside of hammer. Lockplate is plain.

"M" RIFLE

Cal. 58, bbl. 39" with British proof marks; Enfield pattern; tang of trigger guard "L.S.M." Rear sight soldered to bbl.; lockplate (front of hammer) "1862" (rear of hammer) shield with letter "M" and a spread eagle.

Possibly Marshall Manufacturing Company of Holly Springs, Miss.; also known as W. S. McElwaine & Company; Jones, McElwaine & Company. The partners were W. S. McElwaine, W. A. P. Jones, Capt. E. G. Barney, J.

H. Athey. Conf. government bought plant in 1862 and moved machinery to Macon, Georgia.

MENDENHALL, JONES & GARDNER RIFLE

Deep River, Old Jamestown, N. C.

Cal. 58, bbl. 33″, iron butt plate, brass trigger guard. Lockplate (forward of hammer) "M. J. & G., N. C." (rear of hammer) "C.S. 1863."

Firm consisted of Cyrus P. Mendenhall, Ezekiel P. Jones and Grafton Gardner of Greensboro, N. C.

MORSE BREECH-LOADING ALTERED MUSKET

Cal. 69, bbl. 40½″, stock 43″, U. S. model 1831 altered to breech-loading; the top of bbl. is cut out and hinged breech action inserted; hammer cut down to cocking piece. Lockplate m. "U. S. spread eagle, Springfield 1839" George W. Morse, nephew of Samuel Morse, invented this breech-loader to use metallic self-primed cartridges. Morse was Superintendent of the Tennessee Armory (Nashville, Tenn.). The machinery was moved to Chattanooga, then to Atlanta, and then to Greenville, S. C. where arms were made for S. C.

MORSE BREECH-LOADING CARBINE

Greenville, S. C.

Cal. 50, bbl. 20″, no markings except serial numbers; brass frame and ramrod tubes; butternut stock; hinged breech action.

MURRAY CARBINE, MUSKETOON

Columbus, Ga.

Eldridge S. Greenwood and William C. Gray formed firm of Greenwood & Gray to back J. P. Murray, gunsmith.

Cal. 58, bbl. 24″ all brass mounted lockplate "J. P. Murray, Columbus, Ga." Breech m. "Ala. 1864" and F.C.H.", initials of Major F. C. Humphries, Ordance inspector.

MURRAY RIFLE

Cal. 58, bbl. 32¾″, lockplate "J. P. Murray, Columbus, Ga." Breech m. "Ala. & year & F.C.H."

MURRAY SHARPSHOOTER'S RIFLE

Cal. 50, bbl. 29″, bbl. thick and octagon shape; wooden ramrod.

"P" BREECH-LOADING CARBINE

Allegedly made in Tallassee, Alabama

Cal. 52, bbl. 22½″, iron breechblock, bronze-lined, with spiral groove to seat cartridge tightly. Very well made. Partially follows Perry carbine pattern and partially Maynard pattern. Marked "P" on breechblock.

"P" RIFLED CARBINE (HODGKINS CARBINE)

Cal. 58, bbl. 22″, U. S. Model 1854 iron mountings except brass tip foreend; swivel ramrod. bbl. m. "P.C.S.A." Inside of lock m. "C 44". Allegedly made by D. C. Hodgkins & Son, Macon, Georgia. $70

PULASKI RIFLE

Pulaski, Tennessee

Cal. 58, bbl. 32¼″, brass mountings, pattern U. S. Model 1841. Marked "Pulaski, T.C.S.A. 61"

RICHMOND CARBINE

Cal. 58, bbl. 25″, 2 bands; 3 sling swivels, bronze butt plate m. "C.S.", bbl. m. year C.S. lockplate "C.S. Richmond plus year."

RICHMOND NAVY MUSKETOON

Cal. 62, bbl. 30″; follows pattern U. S. Model 1855. Lockplate. "C.S. Richmond, Va. plus year."

RICHMOND RIFLED MUSKET

Richmond, Va. mfgd. with machinery removed from Harper's Ferry. Cal. 58, bbl. 40″; close copy of U. S. Model 1855; brass butt plate. Lockplate (forward end) m. "C. S. Richmond, Va." (read end) m. "Year" bbl. marked with year. $40

ROBINSON-SHARPS CARBINE
Richmond, Va.

Cal. 50, bbl. 21½", copy of Sharps without priming magazine, poor quality. Lockplate m. "S. C. Robinson Arms Mfg. Co., Richmond, Va. Year plus serial number." Marking on bbl. similar to lockplate.

STURDIVANT RIFLE

Cal. 54, bbl. 32", small stock, all brass mounting, no marks except serial number. Mfgd. by Lewis G. Sturdivant of Talladega, Alabama.

TALLASSEE MUZZLE-LOADING CARBINE
Tallassee, Ala.

Cal. 58, bbl. 25", brass clamping bands, trigger guard and butt plate; swivel ramrod. Plate (forward of hammer) "S.C. Tallassee, Ala." in 3 lines (rear of hammer) "year"

Tallassee Armory utilized machinery and workmen brought from Richmond, Va.

TANNER RIFLE
Bastrop, Texas

Cal. 54, bbl. 33", pattern of Miss. rifle; poor workmanship; about 250 manufactured by N. B. Tanner; serial numbers are the only markings.

TARPLEY CARBINE
Greensboro, N. C.

Cal. 52, paper cartridge, bbl. 23", breechblock swings to the left when the catch spring on the right is opened; iron buttplate; brass breech.

Tang m. "J. H. Tarpley's Patent Feb. 14, 1863"; stock stamped, "Manufactured by J. & F. Garrett & Co. Greensboro, N. C.," also "C.S.A."

TEXAS-ENFIELD RIFLE
Tyler, Texas

Cal. 57, bbl. 33", close copy of En-field rifle, brass mountings, 2-leafed rear sight, bayonet lug, lock attached to stock with only one screw. Lockplate (forward of hammer) m. "Texas Rifle, Tyler, Cal. 57" in three lines (rear of hammer) "C.S." bbl. & butt plate tang m. "C.S."

TODD RIFLED MUSKET
Montgomery, Ala.

Cal. 58, bbl. 40", brass mounted. Lockplate (forward of hammer) "Geo. H. Todd, Montgomery, Ala." (rear of hammer) "C.S.A. 1864."

WALLIS RIFLE
Talladega, Alabama

Daniel Wallis had contract in 1862 with state of Alabama for 1000 Mississippi rifles described as follows: "Of the value and description of the Miss. rifles . . . excepting the bayonet . . . is not to be grooved, and with regulation tube lock and bore with mountings similar to said Mississippi rifles with the exception of the patch box."

WHITNEY ENFIELD-MISS. RIFLE

Cal. 61, bbl. 33", stock 44", close copy Enfield model 1858, iron butt plate; brass trigger guard; bbl. has heavy lug for saber bayonet; knife-blade front sight; single-leaf elevation, rear sight. Lockplate "E. Whitney."

60 were delivered on a sample contract with the State of Mississippi. The contract was cancelled by Mississippi because they were found to be assembled from old parts and not in accord with the terms which designated U. S. Model 1841 as the pattern.

WHITNEY RIFLED MUSKET

Regulation U. S. model 1855 except has brass butt plate, plus unmarked bbl., and lock similar to those made Richmond Armory. Lockplate m. "E. Whitney, New Haven."

WYTHEVILLE—HALL MUZZLE —LOADING RIFLE

Wytheville, Va.

Cal. 54, made at Wytheville with parts from Harper's Ferry except for lock stock, hand-made; one piece brass casting with center-hung hammer converts breech-loader to muzzle-loader.

COFER REVOLVER

Cal. 36 perc., 6 shot, 7″ rifled bbl. m. "T. W. Cofer's Patent, Portsmouth, Va.," brass frame. Confederate Patent Office issued a patent for this revolver to Thomas W. Cofer, August 12, 1861.

COLUMBUS REVOLVER

Cal. 36 perc., 6 shot, 7½″ round bbl. m. "Columbus Fire Arms Manuf. Co., Columbus," Trigger guard plate m. "C.S.", serial number on various parts. Brass trigger guard, front sight, and handle strap.

Mfgd. at Columbus, Georgia by Louis and Elias Haiman doing business under the firm style of Columbus Fire Arms Manufacturing Company.

DANCE REVOLVER

Cal. 44 perc., 6 s., 8″ round also 8″ octagon bbl., rifled, brass trigger guard, back strap and blade front sight; iron frame, no recoil shield.

Dance Brothers consisted of James Henry Dance, James P., David, and Claudius. They employed Jesse Parks and his brother, Anderson. The Dance Brothers plant was at Columbia, Texas. War changes forced them to move plant to Grimes County, 3 miles north of Anderson, Texas.

DANCE NAVY REVOLVER

Cal. 36 perc., 6 shot, 7⅜″ part octagon bbl., iron frame, no recoil shield.

GRISWOLD & GRIER REVOLVER

Cal. 36 perc., 6 s., 7½″ rifled bbl., brass frame; only marks are serial numbers on frame, bbl. & cylinder.

Referred to as "Brass-frame Confederate Colt."

Mfgd. at Griswoldville near Macon, Georgia, by Giles G. Griswold, who died, and factory managed by E. C. Grier his brother-in-law. The firm is also referred to as Griswold & Gunnison.

LEECH & RIGDON REVOLVER

Cal. 36 perc., 6 s., 7½″ rifled bbl. m. "Leech & Rigdon" or "Leech & Rigdon, C.S.A." Some are without name identification and some are with name identification but omit C.S.A. Brass front sight, trigger guard and handle strap.

Charles H. Rigdon & Thomas Leech in April 1862 formed partnership at Memphis, Tenn., that traded as both Memphis Novelty Works and Thomas Leech & Co. They manufactured swords. War changes compelled them to move to Columbus, Miss., in May 1862. War changes in December 1862 compelled them to move to Greensboro, Ga. They received a contract for revolvers in March 1863 and in December 1863 the partnership was dissolved. (see Rigdon, Ansley & Company)

RIGDON & ANSLEY REVOLVER

Cal. 36 perc., 6 s., 7½″ rifled bbl. m. "Augusta, Ga. C.S.A. plus serial number." Some markings omit Augusta, Ga., and have only C.S.A. plus serial number. Brass trigger guard, front sight and back strap. Serial number on various parts. Has 12 cylinder stops, a safety device of Manhattan Arms Company of Newark, N. J. (See Leech & Rigdon). Rigdon moved to Augusta, Ga., and in Jan. 1864 organized Rigdon, Ansley & Company. This partnership included Jesse A. Ansley, A. J. Smythe, and C. R. Keen.

Re: 12 cylinder stops: This extra slot in the periphery of the cylinder did away with the pins. It released the strain on the cylinder bolt—stop spring. It provided a safety as it locked the cylinder with the hammer between capped cones.

The Colt revolver had a hole in the hammer face which caught on a pin that projected from the rear face of the cylinder between the cones. The hole in the hammer later was changed to a slot. Hole or slot, the pins were easily damaged because of the strain when the hammer was down on the pin.

SCHNEIDER & GLASSICK REVOLVER

Cal. 36 perc., 6 s., 7½" oct. bbl. brass frame, backstrap and trigger guard. bbl. m. "Schneider & Glassick, Memphis, Tenn." Also model on iron frame with 7½" pt. oct. pt. rd. bbl.

SHERRARD & TAYLOR REVOLVER

(Tucker & Sherrod)

Lancaster, Texas

Cal. 44 perc., 7½" pt. oct. rifled bbl., no marks. Serial numbers on parts. No loading aperture on right side. Close copy of Colt. In July 1862 Tucker, Sherrard & Co. obtained a contract from Texas for the manufacture of 44 and 36 caliber revolvers patterned on Colt's revolver. Tucker, Sherrard & Co. was organized to obtain an arms manufacturing contract and consisted of Lebon Elihu Tucker, A. W. Tucker, Pleasant Taylor, W. L. Killen and J. H. Sherrard. The state papers referred to the firm as Tucker, Sherrod & Co. In August 1862 the firm became Sherrard, Taylor & Co. and so remained until the contract was cancelled in 1863. A. S. Clark, a foreman, in lieu of money received unassembled revolvers' parts and out of these parts after the war came mongrel Clark revolvers. L. E.

Tucker & Son were gun dealers in Marshall, Texas, before the war and it was a practice to stamp dealers' names on guns they sold.

(Used in Confederate Army only by private sale)

SPILLER & BURR REVOLVER

Cal. 36 perc., 6 s., 7" rifled oct. bbl. m. "Spiller & Burr," "C.S." marked on parts; brass frame, resembles a Whitney, some unmarked.

Edward N. Spiller and David J. Burr formed partnership in Richmond, Va., leased building but before manufacturing was begun, moved to Atlanta, Ga. In 1864 Confederate government bought factory.

FAYETTEVILLE PISTOL-CARBINE

Cal. 58, 12" rd. rifled bbl., s.s., model 1855 pistol-carbine with detachable shoulder stock except lockplate is reduced reproduction of Fayetteville rifle. Lockplate m. "Fayetteville" with spread eagle over "C.S.A."

Probably assembled from captured Harper's Ferry parts.

RICHMOND PISTOL

Cal. 54, 10" rd. bbl., brass band & butt plate, swivel ramrod; apparently repaired U. S. arm. U. S. Model 1842 lockplate "C. S. Richmond, Va."

SUTHERLAND PISTOL

Cal. 60 perc., s.s., 6¼" oct. brass bbl. lockplate, "Sutherland, Richmond." French flintlock converted to perc.

TODD REVOLVER

George Todd, a gunsmith, moved to Austin, Texas, from Alabama in 1851. In 1856 when Colt's patent expired he began the manufacture of imitation Colt revolvers patterned after the old Navy model. When Tucker and Sherrard received their revolver contract at the beginning of the war, Todd was induced to go to Lancaster, Texas, where he was slated to become manager of the plant. It is presumed Crockett promised him this. But A. S. Clark, brother-in-law of Pleasant Taylor, one of the owners of the factory, became the manager instead. Todd did not find the terms or the arrangement suitable and went on to the Alabama Armory.

Todd revolvers have steel frames though brass ones have been described but not found.

Unique in Confederate firearm classification are the LeMat inventions. A description in the 1862 Confederate Field Manual states: "Grapeshot pistol—this pistol is manufactured by M. LeMat of Paris. It has a cylinder which revolves, containing 9 chambers, a rifled barrel and a smooth-bore barrel. The latter receives a charge of buckshot, and is fired by a slight change in the hammer."

The rifled barrel was 42 caliber and the under smooth-bore barrel was for 60 caliber shell.

In New Orleans, Louisiana, lived Dr. Jean Alexander Francois LeMat, a physician who, as a hobby, had invented the percussion "grapeshot revolver" and had United States patents granted in 1856 and British patents issued in 1859. Upon formation of the Confederate government and the beginning of the war Dr. LeMat offered his inventions to the Confederacy. They were accepted and Dr. LeMat was given a contract for 5,000 revolvers.

Since he could not find a manufactuer with adequate facilities in the South he took passage for France in an effort to have the weapon manufactured. He sailed on the English mail liner Trent with Mason and Slidell. Stopped by a Federal warship, Mason and Slidell were taken prisoners, but Dr. LeMat was not captured.

In Paris, Dr. LeMat entered into a partnership with C. Girard & Son of 9, Passage Joinville to manufacture the revolvers. Later the Confederate Navy gave him a contract apparently for a caliber 35 with a caliber 50 shot barrel, with inspection in London. Only a few were manufactured under this contract and it was cancelled.

Several models of the LeMat revolvers may be identified.

1. Round barrels, loading levers on right side, spur trigger guard, marked "LeMat's Patent." $700.00

2. Same as No. 1 but marked, "Col. LeMat's Patent." $700.00

3. Similar but loading lever on left side, no spur on trigger guard, marked, "Col. LeMat, bte, s.g.d.g. Paris," which means manufactured for the inventer. $700.00

4. Same as No. 3 but marked, "Syst. LeMat, Bte, s.g.d.g., Paris." $700.00

5. Same but English proof-marks and m. "LeMat & Girard's Patent, London." $700.00

The LeMat pinfire revolver was not a Confederate weapon since it was manufactured post war.

The LeMat Revolving Carbine was a Confederate arm. It was: Caliber 42, percussion, 20½″ part octagon barrel, loading lever on left, ramrod on right, 9-shot cylinder, underbarrel 60 caliber shot. No marks of identification except serial number on frame, cylinder and other parts.

The major defect of LeMat firearms was that they could not take the regulation 44 caliber cartridge.

CONFEDERATE STATES PATENTS

Patents were issued for 13 small arm inventions.

Alexander, C. W., Moorfield, Va.—April 18, 1863—b-l
Clanton, A. J. & T. O., Panola, Miss.—Oct. 3, 1862—b-l
Cofer, Thomas E., Portsmouth, Va.—Aug. 12, 1861—r-f
George, Asa, Charlotte, N. C.—June 10, 1863—r-f
Henry, George, Columbus, Miss.—Sept. 27, 1862—b-l
Howlett, J. W., Greensboro, N. C.—May 10, 1862—b-l
Laquequist, Carl, Macon, Georgia—Jan. 21, 1862—b-l
Legden, A. Atlanta, Georgia—Mar. 10, 1863—r-f
Ligon, E. T., Demopolis, Ala.—Sept. 24, 1861—b-l
Morse, Thomas, Richmond, Va.—Sept. 10, 1863—b-l
Read, N. T., Danville, Va.—March 20, 1863—b-l
Tarpley, J. H., Greensboro, N. C.—Feb. 14, 1863—b-l
White, John, Jr., Citronville, Ala.—Dec. 7, 186—r-f

* b-l.—breech loader; r-f—revolving firearm

Bradbury's Foundry at Port Lavaca, Texas, had a gunsmith department. Here was employed E. C. Singer, a nephew of I. M. Singer of the sewing machine. D. Bradbury wrote to the Texas Military Board that Singer had invented a "marvelous rifle gun" that fired "four minie balls extremely accurate." Nothing further is known of this invention.

The Confederate Ordnance Manual of 1862 lists the following Confederate Ordnance Depots:

Alabama—Mobile, Montgomery, Mt. Vernon, Selma
Georgia—Augusta, Columbus, Macon
North Carolina—Fayetteville, Wilmington
Mississippi—Briarsfield Armory
South Carolina—Charleston
Tennessee—Knoxville
Virginia—Lynchburg, Richmond

CLARK, SHERRARD CO.

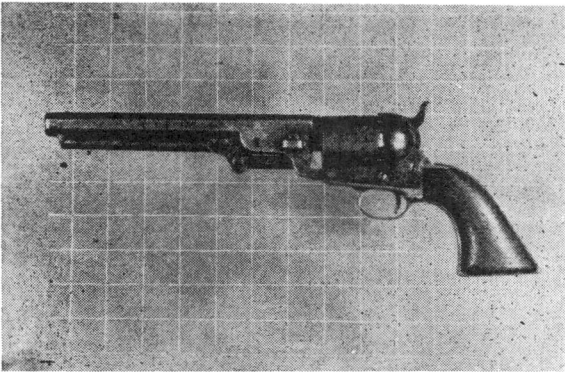

COLUMBUS FIRE ARMS CO.

RIGDON-ANSLEY

ANDERSON PISTOL—ANDERSON, TEXAS

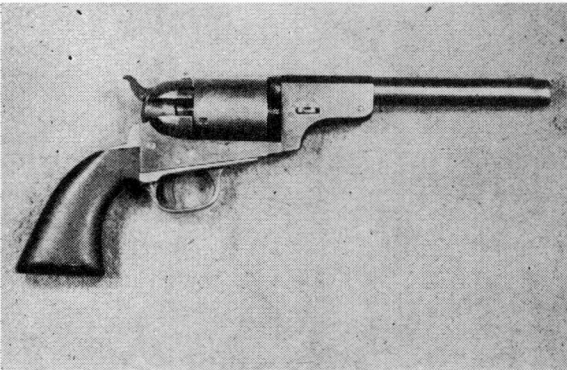

CLARK-SHERRARD

DANCE BROS.

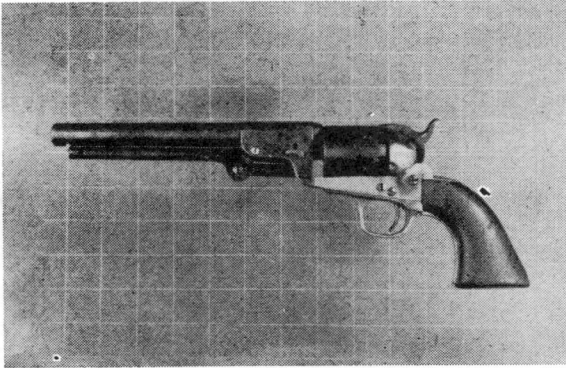

GRISWOLD & GREER

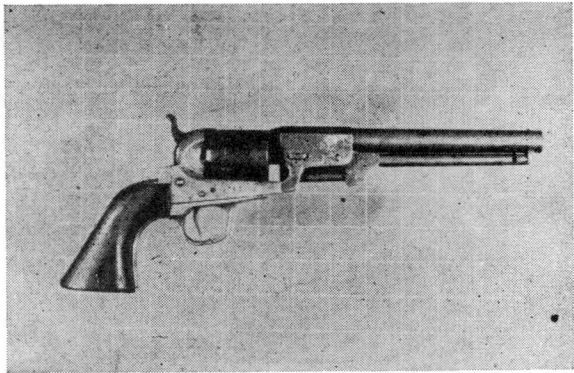

GRISWOLD & GREER

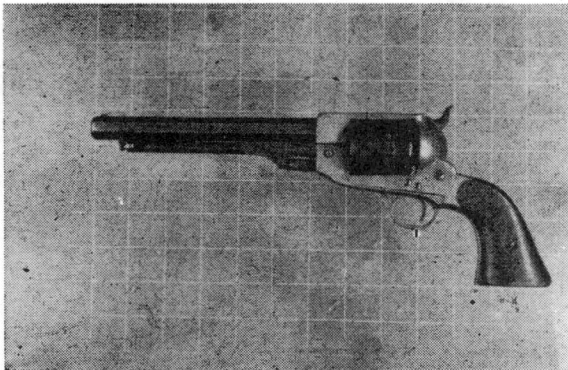

SPILLER & BURR

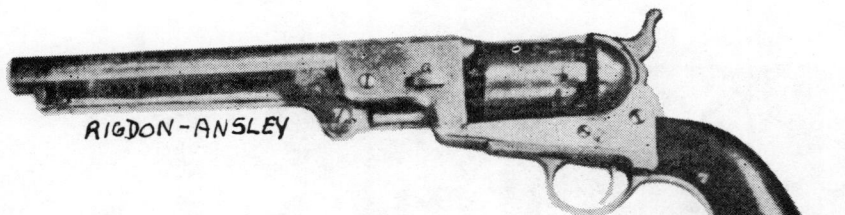

RIGDON-ANSLEY

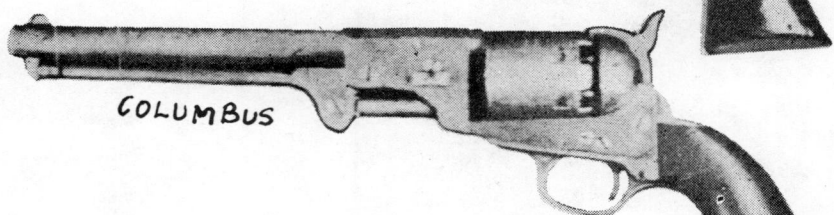

COLUMBUS

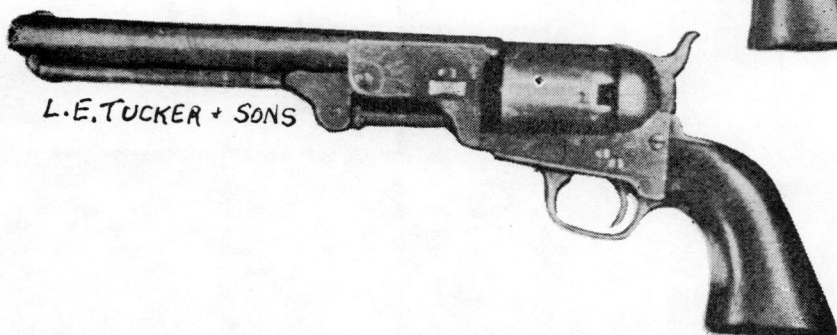

L.E.TUCKER & SONS

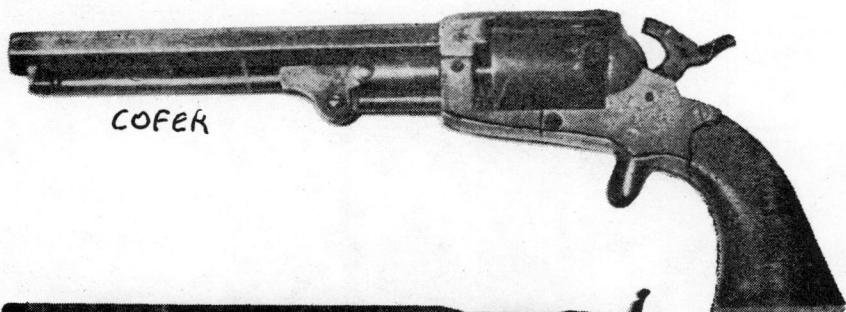

COFER

SCHNEIDER &
GLASSICK

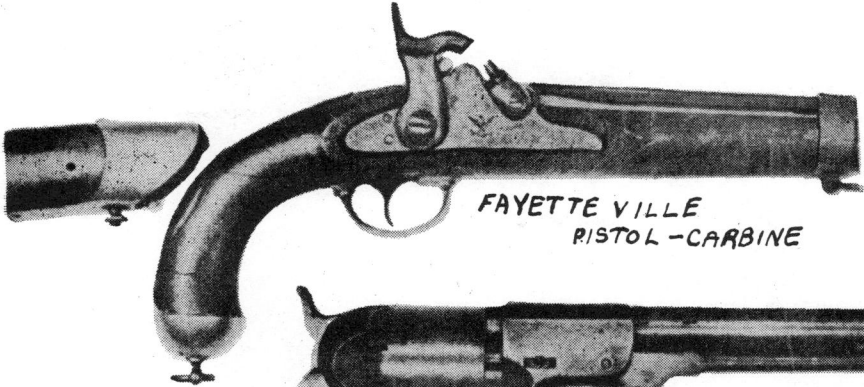

FAYETTE VILLE
PISTOL—CARBINE

LEECH & RIGDON

SPILLER & BURR

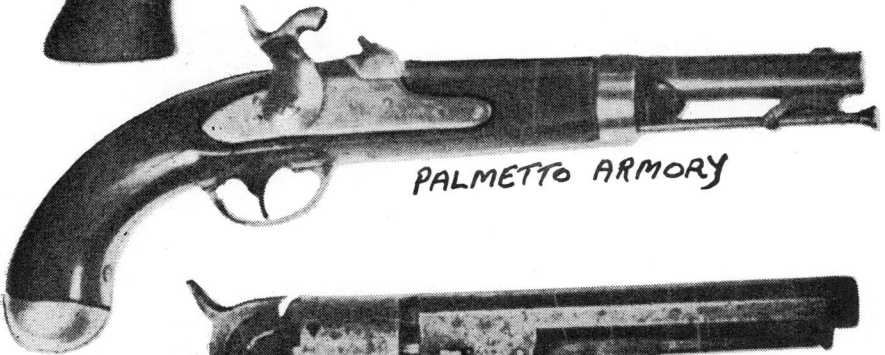

PALMETTO ARMORY

TUCKER & SHERROD

LE MAT

DANCE BROTHERS

GRISWOLD - GRIER

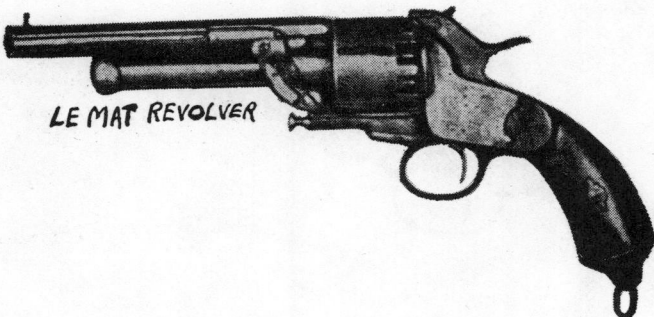

LE MAT REVOLVER

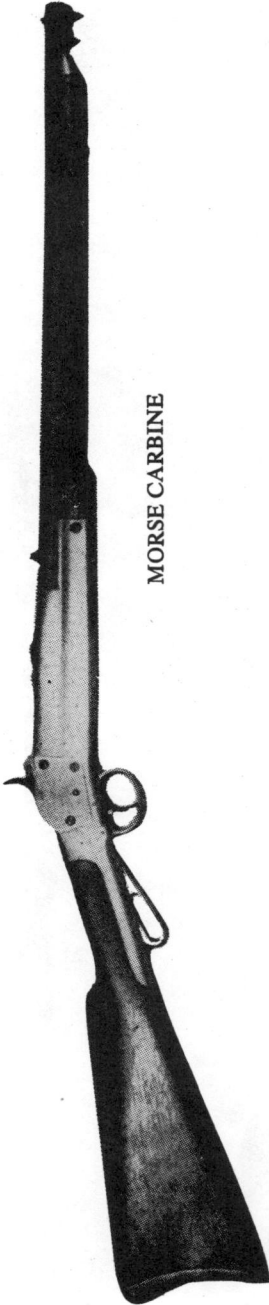

MORSE CARBINE

ENFIELD RIFLE (TYLER, TEXAS)

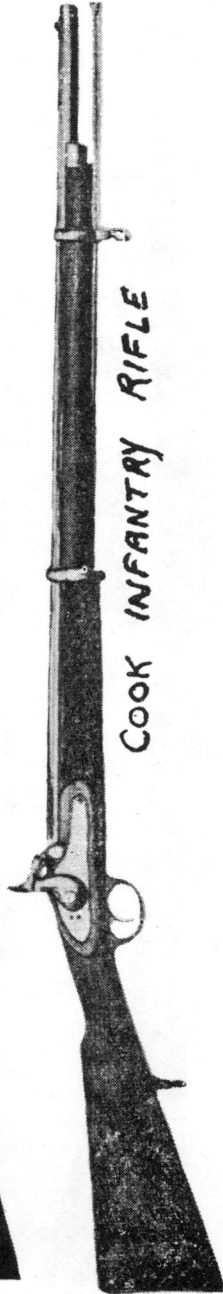

COOK INFANTRY RIFLE

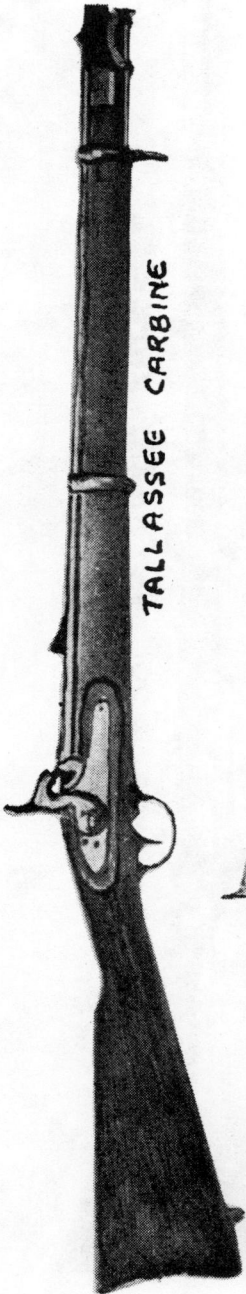

TALLASSEE CARBINE

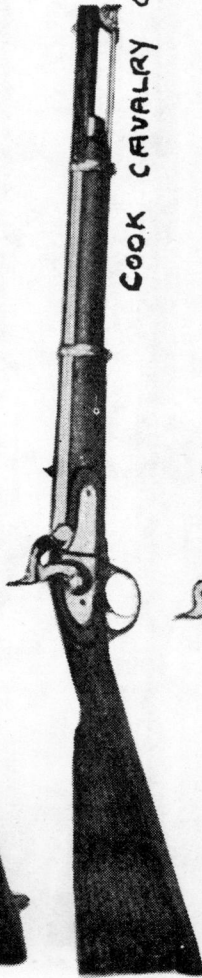

COOK CAVALRY CARBINE

AUSTRIAN RIFLE (TYLER, TEXAS)

TEXAS TRYON

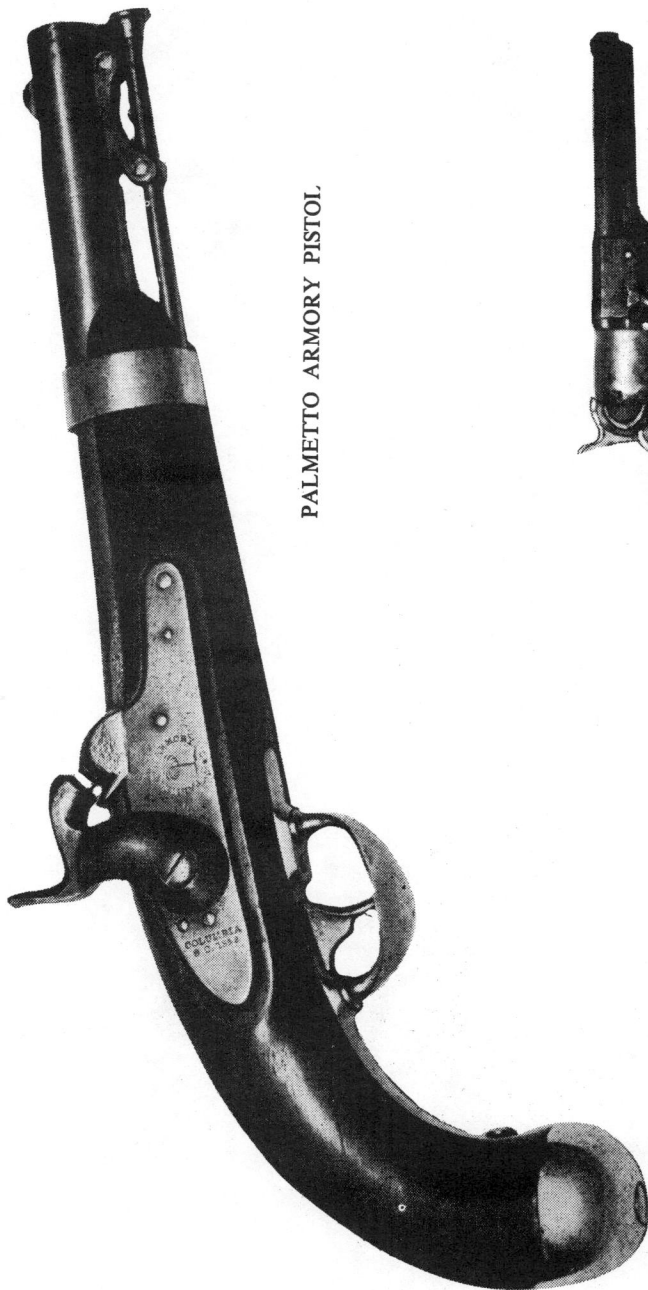

PALMETTO ARMORY PISTOL.

TODD REVOLVER

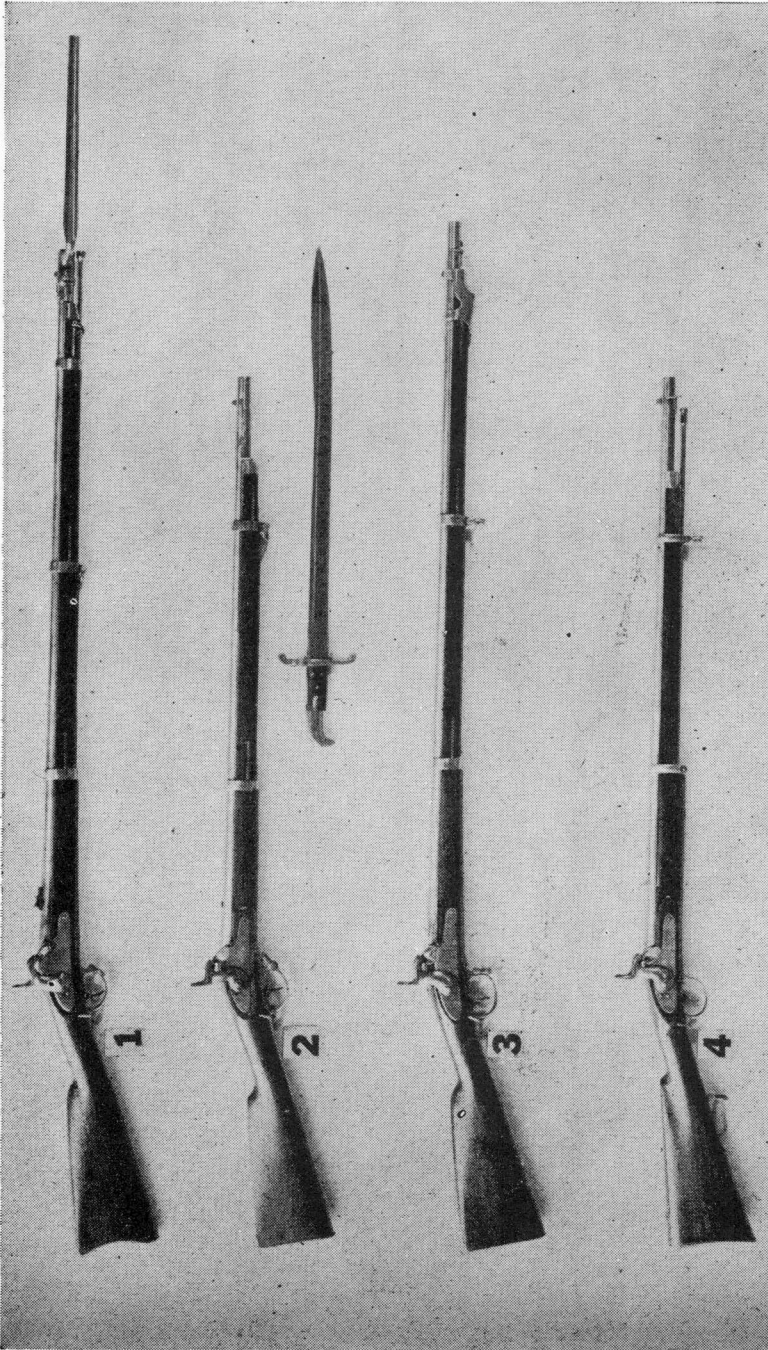

1—CONFEDERATE MUSKET: Smoothbore; Caliber .58; 39½″ barrel; total length, 56″. Marked: lockplate, "C. S. Richmond, Va."; barrel, V. P. eagle's head 1863. Bright finish; Triangular bayonet. —41930-B.

2—CONFEDERATE NORTH CAROLINA RIFLE: Rifled; caliber .56; 32½″ barrel; total length, 48½″. Marked: lockplate, "M.J. & G N. C.," behind hammer, "1864 C. S."; barrel "N.C.P. Brass furniture. Sword bayonet, 24″ blade, total length, 29″ marked ————, War Dept. 222330.

3—PALMETTO MUSKET: Smoothbore; caliber .69; 42″ barrel; total length, 58″.

Marked: lockplate, palm tree, "Palmetto Armory S * C, Columbia, S. C., 1852; barrel "W. G. & Co., V P"; on tang, "S.C.," on butt plate, "S.C." Bright finish. Navy Dept. 256991.

4—CONFEDERATE COOK MUSKET: Smoothbore: caliber .58; 33″ barrel; total length, 48¼″. Marked: "Cook & Brothers, Athens, Ga., 1864 5620." Confederate flag behind hammer; barrel marked same as lock. Brass furniture. Navy Dept. 257062.

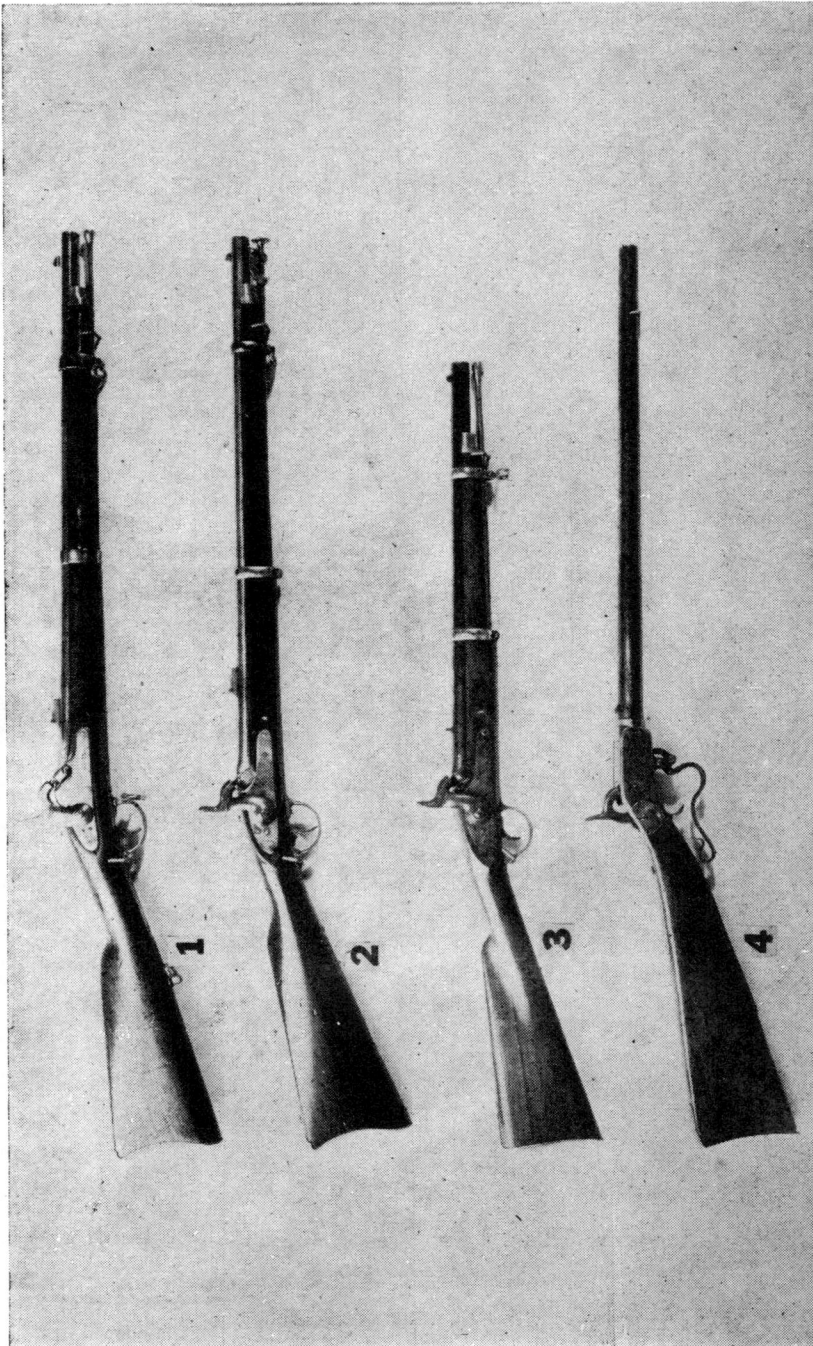

1—CONFEDERATE CARBINE: Smoothbore; caliber .58; barrel, 25''; total length, 41''. Marked: "C. S. Richmond, Va., 1863''; barrel "V P'' eagle's head; butt tang, "U. S.'' War Department.

2—CONFEDERATE TALLASSEE CARBINE: Smoothbore; caliber .58; barrel 25''; total length, 34½''. Marked: "C. S. Tallassee, Ala.'' Brass furniture.

3—COOK CARBINE: Rifled; caliber .58; barrel, 19''; total length, 35''; Lockplate marked, "Cook & Brothers, Athens, Ga., 1864 6130''; flag behind hammer.

Barrel marked same as lock, left side "Proved.'' Rolled bromed barrel. Brass furniture. War Dept. 222395.

4—CONFEDERATE "PERRY OR MAYNARD'' BREECHLOADING CARBINE: Rifled; caliber .52; barrel, 22½''; total length, 40½''. No marks other than letters "I G S'' scratched on lock frame. Brass receiver and frame. War Department 222397.

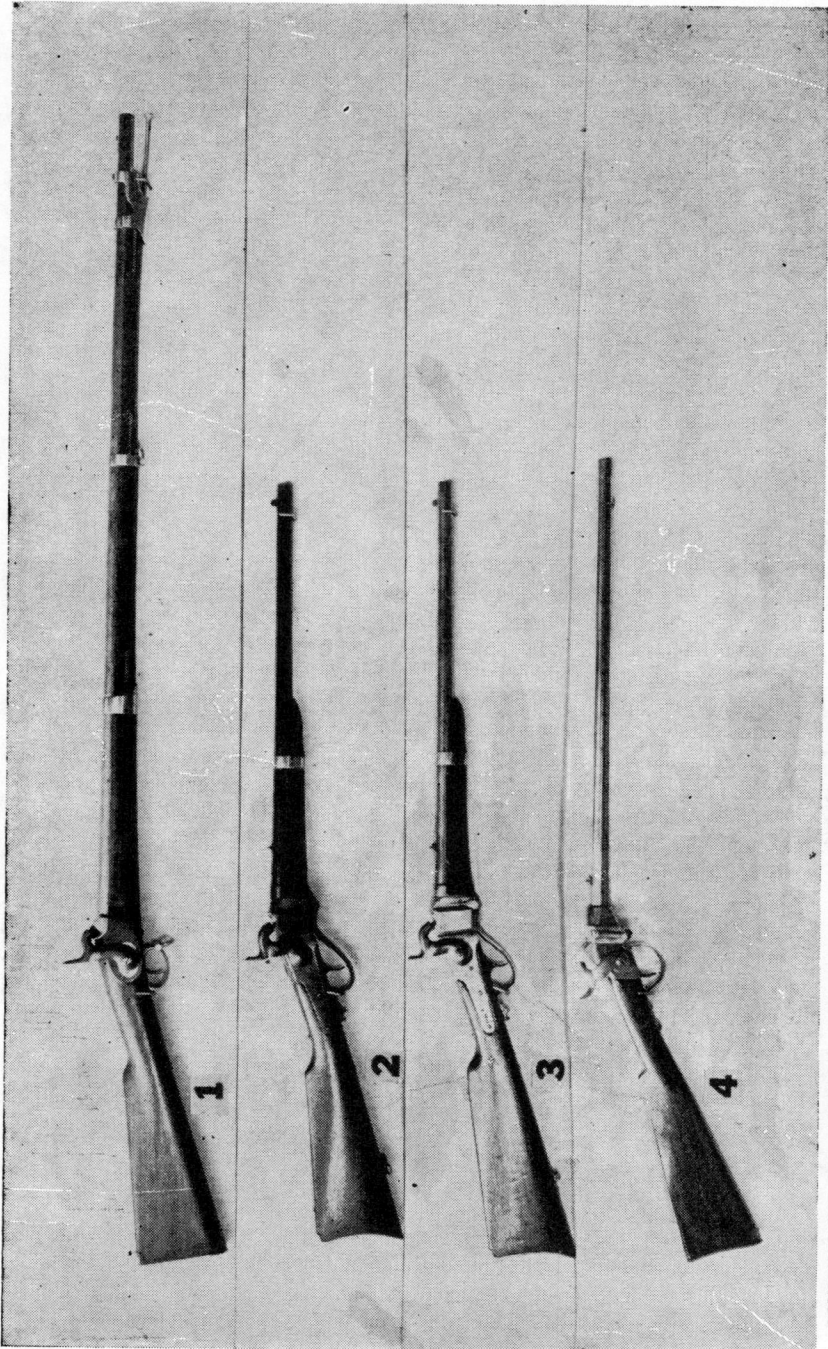

1—CONFEDERATE MORSE MUSKET: Smoothbore; caliber .71; barrel, 43''; total length, 58''; Marked: triggerguard, "Morse's Lock, State Works, Greenville, S. C. 118''. Brass triggerguard; blued hammer. All other furniture bright. War Department 222321.

2—CONFEDERATE ROBINSON CARBINE (IMITATION OF SHARPS) Rifled; caliber .53; barrel 21½''; total length, 38''. Side plate marked: "S. C. Robinson Arms manufactory. Richmond, Va. 1862''; breech tang, "138''. Brass bands and butt plate. War Dept. 222394.

3—CONFEDERATE IMITATION SHARPS CARBINE: Rifled; caliber .58; 20½'' barrel; total length, 38½''. Marked: "Richmond, Va. 2492." Ordnance Dept.

4—CONFEDERATE TARPLEY'S CARBINE: Rifled; caliber .48; 23½'' barrel; total length, 40''. Marked on breech tang "J. H. Tarpley's Pat. Feb. 14, 1863''; barrel marked, "143''; breech block "113." War Dept. 222396.

GRISWOLD & GREER, cal. 36, 6 shot, 7½ inch barrel, brass frame, trigger-guard, and back strap.

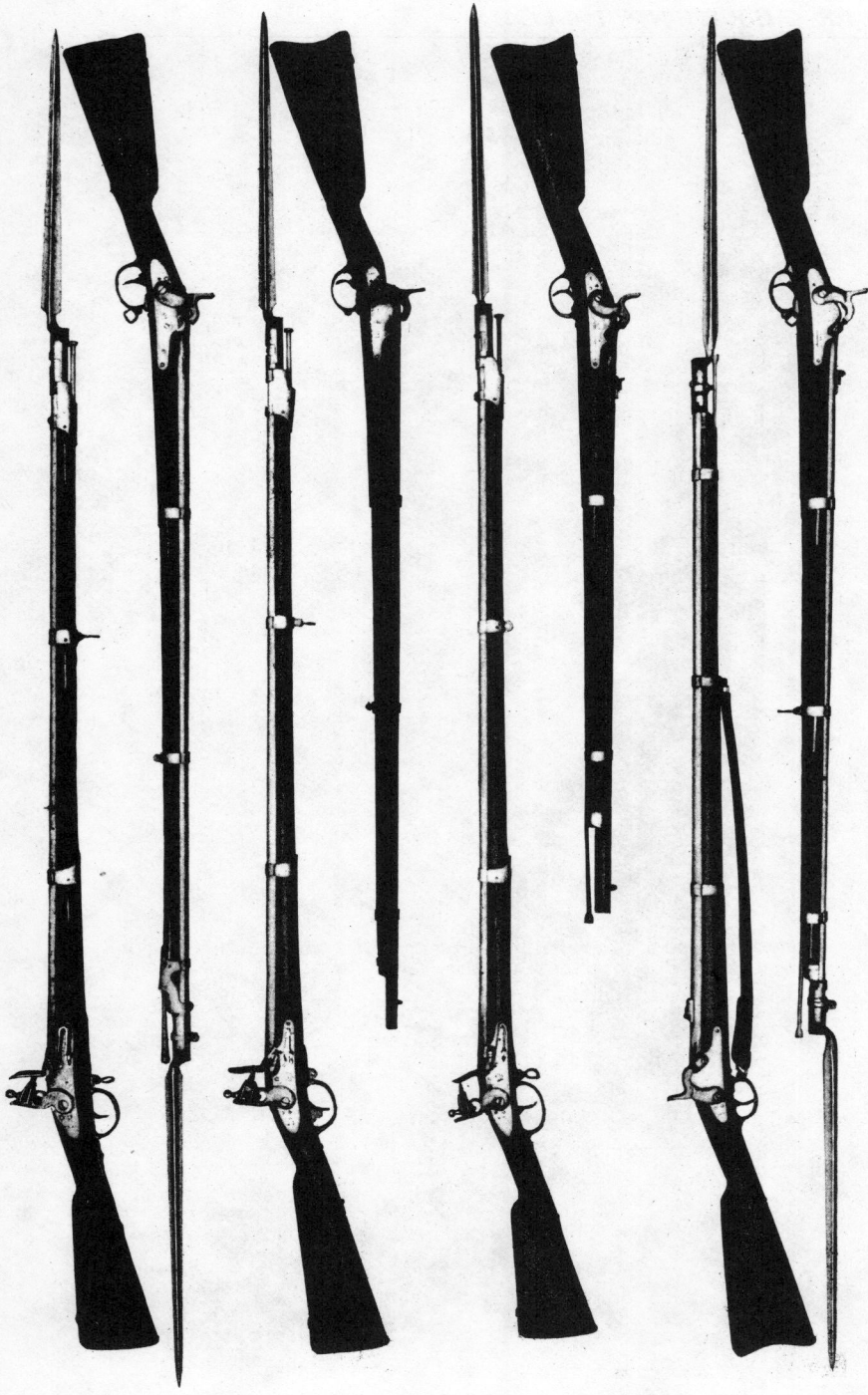

1808 model flint .69-Lock marked, "C.S.A."
1822 model flint 69-lock "C.S." "North Carolina."
1808 .69 "C.S." on lock; stock, "28 Reg. South Carolina."
Conf. Musket .58 perc. tape-lock blank.
1842 .69 perc.

Conf. musket .59 perc. Lock, "1863" "C.S." "Richmond, Va."
Conf. rifle .58 perc. lock, "1863" "C.S.A." "Fayetteville"
Conf. musket .58 perc. "1863" "C.S." "Richmond, Va."
Original Maynard Primer lockplate.

Confederate Weapons

1. U.S. 1808 flint-lock musket. Cal. 69. Lock marked "C.S.A.," **Between** cock and pan, "S.C.", Barrel marked, "P.M., S.J. 111 I.M. South Carolina. Used at beginning of war.

2. U. S. 1822 flint-lock musket cal. 69-Lock m. "U.S." and "C.S." "North Carolina."

3. U. S. 1808 flint-lock musket cal. 69 Lock marked, "J. State," an eagle, "New Haven" "C.S." Stock marked, "28th Reg. South Carolina."

4. Percussion Rifled musket cal. 58. Lock plate made a primerlock, Model 1855.

5. U. S. 1842 Perc. musket cal. 69. This is first model made Springfield Armory 1850. Owned by Georgia soldier.

6. Percussion Rifled musket, cal. 58. Lock "1863", "C.S.", "Richmond, Va."

7. Percussion Rifle cal. 58. Lock stamped "1863" "C.S.A." under eagle "Fayetteville." Brass mounted.

8. Percussion Rifled musket cal. 58. Lock stamped "1863" "C.S." "Richmond, Va." Originally lock forged for Maynard Primer.

The inventory of the Arsenals at the beginning of the War when they became Confederate property was as follows:

ARSENAL	Perc. Muskets	F-L changed to Perc. Muskets	Perc. Rifles
Charleston, S. C.	9,280	5,720	2,000
Fayetteville, N. C.	15,480	9,520	2,000
Augusta, Ga.	12,380	7,620	2,000
Mt. Vernon, Ala.	9,280	5,720	2,000
Baton Rouge, La.	18,580	11,420	2,000
	65,000	40,000	10,000

Confederate-made rifles are mainly either copies of 1 U. S. Rifle, U. S. Rifle-Musket 1855, 2 U. S. Rifle Model 1841, 3. Enfield.

More than half of all Confederate infantry weapons were made in Richmond, Virginia at the old Virginia Armory. 80% of the 20,000 rifle-muskets roughly were U. S. Rifle 1855 pattern. Produced more than 20,000 rifle-muskets, more than 1,000 muskets, more than 2,500 carbines or a total of 27,370. In addition they assembled 12,212 shoulder arms from parts.

Fayetteville, N. C. Armory produced about 7,000 arms, copies of 1855 U. S. Rifle.

Athens, Ga. Armory (Cook & Brother) produced more than in Athens of the Enfield Rifle, Musketoon and Carbine. Cook Bros. also produced about 1,200 at New Orleans (Marked, "N.O." on lock behind hammer).

Confederate National Armory originally at Asheville, N. C., moved in '63 to Columbia, S. C.—made Model 1841 copies.

Holly Springs, Miss., made few arms and machinery later moved to Macon, Ga.

Tyler, Texas made few arms.

Billups & Son of Mound Prairie made 1841 rifles.

White, Carver, Campbell & Co. of Dusk, Texas made 1841 rifles.

Small shops that made long arms included: Dickson Nelson, Ala. copies 1841 model; Davis & Bozeman, Ala. copies 1841; Greenwood & Gray, Columbus, Ga., 1841 copies; Pulaski, Tenn., (Marked "Pulaski" "1861") 1841 copies; Ga. Armory, 1841 copies; Mendenhall, Jones & Gardner, N. C., 1841 copies.

Definite proof is lacking but the unusual Confederate muzzle-loader from parts of Hall breech-loader salvaged from Harpers Ferry was assembled by J. B. Barrett of Wytheville, Va. The solid breech is cast brass but the stock is handmade.

Small shops include George W. Kemper of Goodlettsville, Tenn.; and Alexander Stalcup, Goodlettsville, Tenn.

The first machine gun ever to be used successfully in battle was used by the Confederacy, and was the invention of Capt. D. R. Williams of Covington, Ky. Another machine gun was the invention of Gen. Josiah Gorgas, Chief of Ordnance. It was single-barrel, cast-iron, smooth-bore, caliber 1.25 inches.

Directory of Confederate Edged Weapons

Makers, Dealers, Importers.

BAKER, John—Bowie knives for Ga.

BASSONET, L—Mobile, Ala.—made swords

BAYSER, STEBBINS & CO.—Columbia, S. C.—bayonets

BELL & DAVIS—Atlanta, Ga.—Bowie knives

BERRY, Will—Bowie knives for Ga.

BOYLE, GAMBLE & MacFEE—Richmond, Va., made swords; also military outfitters.

BURGER & BRO.—Richmond, Va.—made swords, bayonets, Bowie knives.

CAMERON & WINN—Bowie knives for Ga.

CANFIELD BROTHERS—Balto., Md.— military outfitters.

CHRISTOPHER, C. J.—Atlanta, Ga.— sword maker

CLARKSON, ANDERSON & CO. also CLARKSON & CO.—Richmond, Va.— dealer

COLLEGE HILL ARSENAL—Nashville, Tenn. (L. T. Cunningham) private enterprise—made swords similiar to Sharp & Hamilton, Nashville Plow Works.

COLUMBIA, S .C. (K. G. & K.)—see Kraft, Goldschmidt & Kraft

COLUMBIA ARMORY—(McPhail's Armory) Columbia, S. C.—made sabers

COLUMBUS IRON WORKS—see L. Haiman

CONFEDERATE STATE ARMORY— Kenansville, N. C.—(Louis Froelich & Bernard Estvan) private enterprise. Swordmakers. Guard stamped out of sheet brass. In '62 Froelich became sole owner.

CONNING, James—Mobile, Ala.—made swords & sabers.

COOK & BROS.—Athens, Ga.—see Cook & Co.

COOK & CO.—New Orleans, La. (Ferdinand W. C. Cook & Francis, brothers)— made swords, sabers, bayonets. '62 moved to Athens, Ga.

COURTNEY & TENNANT—Charleston, S. C. (G. B. Tennant)—importer

CRUSH & WADE—Christiansburg, Va.— made sabers

CUNNINGHAM, L. T.—Nashville, Tenn. —see College Hill Arsenal,—made swords.

DELANO, W. J.—Memphis, Tenn.—dealer

DE WITT, Abraham H.—Columbus, Ga.— made swords—see Greenwood & Gray

DRISCOLL, T. D.—Va.—sword maker

DULFINO CO.—New Orleans, La. Sword maker & dealer

EAGLE FOUNDRY—Memphis, Tenn.— (Streeter, Chamberlain & McDaniel)— made sabers

EASTVAN, Bernard—partner Louis Froelich

ETOWAH IRON WORKS—Etowah, Ga.— made Bowie knives.

EYLAND & HAYDEN—importer—see Hayden & Whilden

FORD, J. J.—made Bowie knives

FREEMAN, B. P.—Macon, Ga.—swordmaker—After 1861 worked for E. J. Johnston Co.; W. J. McElroy, both of Macon, Ga.

FROELICH, LOUIS—Wilmington, N. C. Col. Eastvan left firm in '61. Froelich moved to Kenansville, FROELICH & EASTVAN, N. C. There until '63 when factory destroyed by Union forces—made swords & sabers. Used trade name also of CONFEDERATE STATE ARMORY.

GEORGIA ARMORY—Milledgeville, Ga. —1861-64—made sabers, bayonets

GILLILAND, H.—made Bowie knives

GITTER & MOSS—Memphis, Tenn.—made swords

GRAY, John G.—Columbus, Ga.—made Bowie knives & sabers

GRAY, William C.—brother of John & his partner—see Greenwood & Gray

GREEN, Col. John—made sabers

GREENWOOD & GRAY—Columbus, Ga. —(Eldridge S. Greenwood, William C. Gray) later Greenwood, Gray & Dewitt

GREGG, HAYDEN & CO.—Charleston, S.C.—military outfitters since early 1800's. see Hayden & Whilden, Eyland & Hayden

GRISWOLD, THOMAS & COMPANY— New Orleans, La.—military outfitters, succeeded Hyde & Goodrich in '61

HABERSHAM, R. W.—made sabers

HAIL, F. M.—Bowie knives

HAIMAN, ELIAS—Elias & Louis Haiman, Hungarian Jewish emigrants, settled in Columbus.

HAIMAN, L. & BRO.—Ga.—about 1830. They were tinsmiths. They made swords, sabers and also imported weapons. As COLUMBUS IRON WORKS, they manufactured revolvers.

HALFMAN & TAYLOR—Montgomery, Ala.—military outfitters, importers.

HALL, C. —Norfolk, Va.—dealer

HAYDEN, Augustus—Charleston, S.C.— military outfitter—see Hayden & Whilden; also Gregg, Hayden & Co.

HAYNES, O. S.—Bowie knives

HECK, BRODIE & CO.—(J. M. Heck & Max Brodie)—Raleigh, N.C.—also as RALEIGH BAYONET FACTORY— made bayonets

HUGHES, R. J.—Bowie knives

HYDE & GOODRICH—New Orleans— Military outfitters.

ISAACS & CO.—London, England—military outfitters. Swords have ISAACS stamped on

ISAACS, S. CAMPBELL & CO.—back of blade, checkered leather grips, iron guard.

JOHNSTON, E. J. & CO.—Macon, Ga.—made swords

K. G. & K. —(Kraft, Goldschmidt & Kraft)—Columbia, S.C.—made swords. Peter W. & H. F. Kraft, brothers and Isaac Goldschmidt.

KEAN'S SWORD SHOP—Columbus, Ga.—made swords.

KENT, PAINE & CO.—Richmond, Va.—military outfitters

KIND, PETER—Columbia, S.C.—Brass foundry—cast sword guards for K. G. & K.

KNIGHT'S BLACKSMITH SHOP—Amelia, Va.—Bowie knives

LAN & SHERMAN—Richmond, Va.—Bowie knives

LEECH, Thomas S. as MEMPHIS NOVELTY WORKS—made swords. Later with Charles H. Rigdon made revolvers.

MACON ARMORY—Macon, Ga.—Col. James Burton—pistols & swords

MACON ARSENAL—Macon, Ga.—made edged weapons. Conf. Govt. moved Ordnance supplies from Savannah to Macon. D. C. Hodgkins & Co. also Findley Iron Works were purchased and combined into Arsenal.

McELROY, W. J. & CO.—Macon, Ga.—made swords

MARSHALL, H.—Atlanta, Ga.—made swords

McKINSTRY, Alexander—Mobile, Ala.—made Bowie knives

MEMPHIS NOVELTY WORKS—see Leech, Thomas

MICON, B. H.—as TALLAHASSEE ARMORY—at Tallahassee, Ala.—made swords

MITCHELL & TYLER—Richmond, Va.—military outfitter—sold Boyle & Gamble swords with C. S. and star in hilt.

MOLE, Robert & sons—Birmingham, England—swordmakers—still in business

MORRISON, Murdoch—N.C.—Bowie knives

NASHVILLE PLOW WORKS—Nashville, Tenn.— (Sharp & Hamilton). Converted Plow Works into Sword manufacture, reversing biblical admonition. Apr. '62 after Fall of Nashville, manufacture stopped.

RALEIGH BAYONET FACTORY—Raleigh, N.C.—see Heck, Brodie & Co.

RICHMOND, C. & CO.—Memphis, Tenn.—made swords

RIGGINS, Thomas, Supt.—Knoxville Arsenal, Tenn.—made swords

ROBINSON, ADAMS & CO.—Richmond, Va.—dealer

SCHNITZLER & KIRSCHBAUER (S. & K.)—Solengen, Germany—dealers edged weapons

SHARP & HAMILTON—Nashville, Tenn.—see Nashville Plow Works

SMITH, John C.—Bowie knives

STATON, John L.—Virginia—sword maker

TALLAHASSEE ARMORY—see Micon

TREDEGAR IRON WORKS—Richmond. Va. (Joseph R. Anderson)—largest gun foundry in South—made bayonets

WEED, N.—Bowie knives

ZIMMERMAN, J. C. & CO.—Bowie knives

CURRENT PRICES

Asheville Rifle	$ 450.00
Austrian Rifle	225.00
Baker Rifle	275.00
Cook & Brothers Rifle	750.00
Dickson, Nelson Carbine	550.00
Rifle	550.00
Fayetteville Rifle	800.00
Ga. Armory Rifle	550.00
Lamb Rifle	550.00
"M" Rifle	500.00
Morse-B.-L. Musket	650.00
Carbine	800.00
Hodgkins Carbine	500.00
Richmond Carbine	650.00
Navy-Musketoon	600.00
Studivant Rifle	550.00
Tarpley Carbine	700.00
Wytheville-Hall Rifle	650.00

REVOLVERS

Columbus	2000.00
Dance	3000.00
Griswold & Greer	3000.00
Leech & Rigdon	2000.00
Rigdon & Ansley	2750.00
Spiller & Burr	1500.00